TOUCHED BY HANNAH

CHRIS HENNESSY

Touched by Hannah. A man with cancer. His one-pound newborn. And their fight for life.

Published by HennSchtick Productions
Woodland, CA 95695
408-568-9330

Chris Hennessy's HennSchtick Productions is honored to present this book. The views expressed or implied in this work are those of the author. HennSchtick Productions represents design excellence, creative content, integrity, and high-quality productions.

This memoir is a recollection of events whose time, place, and circumstances happened to the best of my memory. I've endeavored to tell my story with transparency, self-reflection, and depth, according to my interpretations and perceptions. Some names have been changed to protect their privacy.

Printed in the United States of America

ISBN: 979-8-9996857-0-4 (Paperback)
ISBN: 979-8-9996857-1-1 (eBook)
LCCN: 2025913137

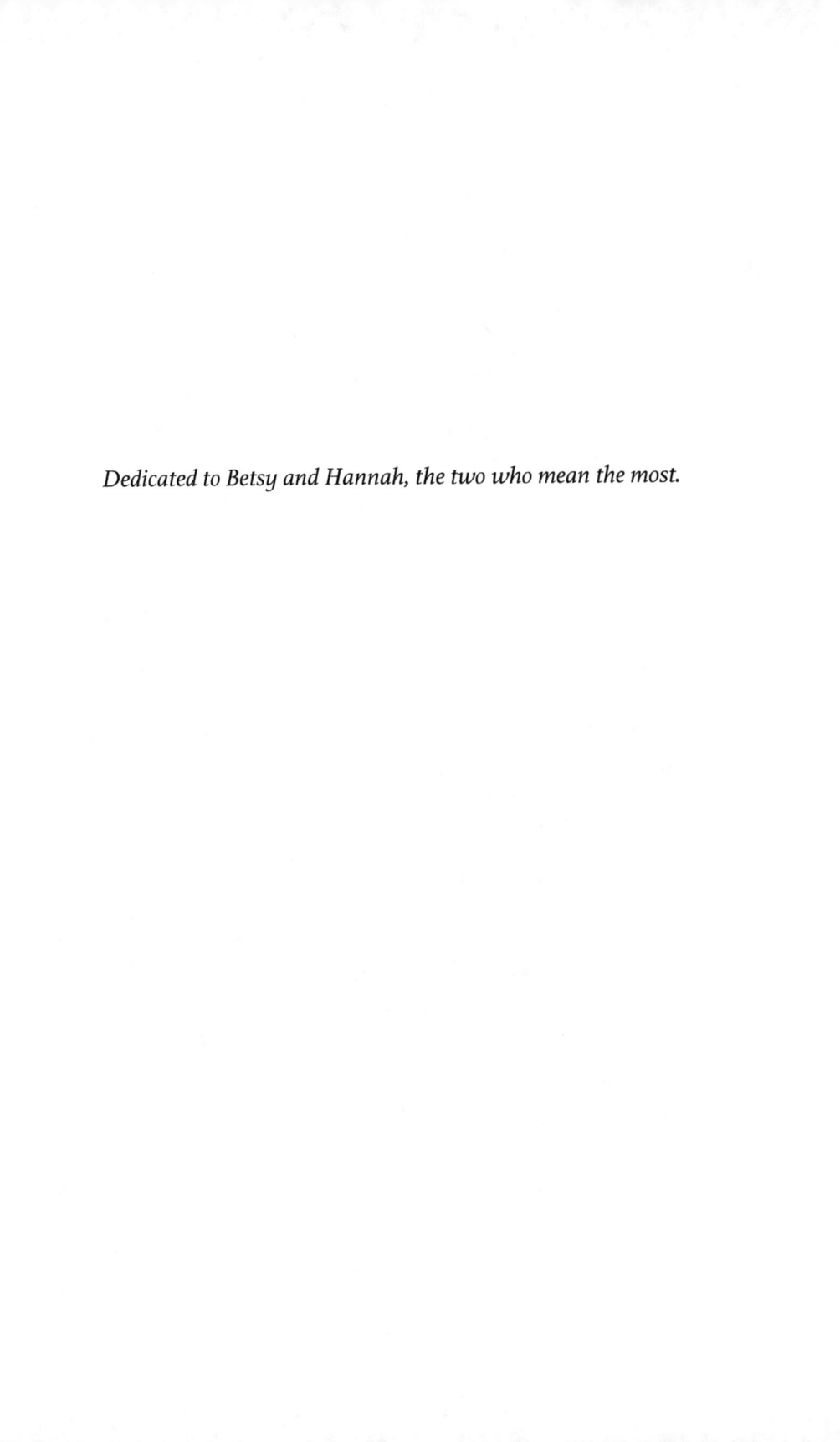

Dedicated to Betsy and Hannah, the two who mean the most.

CONTENTS

FOREWORD

Touched by Hannah could have been written as a sad tale, but Chris Hennessy's resilience and fortitude, paired with his positive attitude and quirky sense of humor, make this a powerful reading experience. He's both an excellent storyteller and an extraordinary person—I was completely hooked in the first five pages.

In 1999, Chris met Betsy at a Whole Foods store while she was studying for a college exam. They talked, and there was not only great attraction, but what followed was a fast, falling-in-love story.

In 2003, they were married, and Chris delivers a hilarious account of the chaos that ensued. Picture this: a locked car with keys inside and engine running, leading to police intervention and an unexpected escort to the wedding.

Chris and Betsy set out to fulfill their longtime dream of having a baby girl they planned to name Hannah.

Three years passed without conception, so they both went for checkups. Chris faced a potential prostate cancer diagnosis after his

PSA blood tests revealed abnormally elevated levels. His doctor explained that if the upcoming biopsy confirmed cancer, both the biopsy itself and the required surgery would cause permanent infertility.

They pleaded with the doctor to allow two months instead of two weeks until the biopsy, still believing and wanting to try one last time for Hannah. On May 17, 2009—sixteen days before Chris's scheduled biopsy—a late-night pregnancy test came back positive. Betsy was miraculously pregnant. The due date was December 7, 2009.

Chris masterfully weaves together the pregnancy section with razor-sharp wit and raw emotion. You'll find yourself caught up in the celebration, ready to dance with your spouse and fall in love all over again. I was laughing out loud—the kind of deep belly laughs that come from perfect comedic timing.

The biopsy was positive for aggressive prostate cancer. Surgery was scheduled for August 3, 2009.

The average age of prostate cancer diagnosis is in the late sixties. Chris is only 52. The doctor tells him, "Attitude is everything. Stay your positive, uplifting, and humorous self."

Chris does.

Hannah was born on September 1, 2009, at twenty-six weeks' gestation and weighed only one pound, nine ounces. Her survival remained touch-and-go. Even if she pulled through, doctors warned of likely developmental challenges ahead.

Hannah was placed in an incubator. Chris or Betsy can stick an arm through the small hole into the incubator and use the index finger to touch their micro-preemie. When Chris reached inside and softly stroked her hand, Hannah grasped his index finger and held on for hours. Chris called it a magical daddy-daughter bonding experience that profoundly impacted his life.

The Hennessys had been members of the vibrant Westgate Church in San Jose, CA, since 2005. In 2007, they began serving as leaders in a children's ministry class for toddlers, offering the children boundless love, compassion, and encouragement. Both the children and their parents embraced the Hennessys wholeheartedly for their dedicated care and nurturing spirit.

After Hannah's birth, members of the Westgate community rallied around Chris and Betsy—a beautiful example of how immersing yourself in community creates a support system that sustains you through life's most severe storms.

Hannah continues to endure one crisis after another, but each time she perseveres and conquers. Chris and Betsy are convinced it's the thousands of prayers from their church and Chris's Facebook community—combined with their unwavering faith and love for Hannah—that are helping her climb required mountains.

"You have a gift that we've never seen in the NICU—joy, laughter, and positivity," Hannah's doctor said to Chris.

Even while writing this book, Chris faced his own staggering life-threatening challenges—including Stage IV prostate cancer that metastasized to his lungs. Still, Chris refused to quit. He *needed* to finish *Touched by Hannah*, and somehow, he did. My respect for both Chris and his remarkable book knows no bounds.

What makes this book truly powerful is the unwavering humor, positive approach, strength, and love of Hannah's parents. The recounting of events remains upbeat and humorous, regardless of the overwhelming problems they face.

Cecil Murphey is the author or co-author of 140 books, including the best sellers Gifted Hands: The Ben Carson Story *and* 90 Minutes in Heaven, *written for Don Piper.*

PROLOGUE

"Betsy, if we hadn't been trying to conceive and gotten those fertility tests—we wouldn't have found my cancer."

That realization hit me in 2012: how our desperate, longtime longing for Hannah—which brought us Hannah—may have saved my life. We did conceive, miraculously, but nothing could have prepared us for what followed—Hannah's arrival at just 26 weeks, weighing one pound, nine ounces.

Three years had passed since 2009, the year that tried to break us —Hannah's birth and my aggressive prostate cancer diagnosis and surgery. I finally understood that this was a film I had to make.

When I reached out to fellow producers in the Northern California film community, the response was unanimous. "This was uncharted territory." "A story that needs to be told."

One conversation stood out. Producer Frank Jones leaned forward with the intensity I'd seen him bring to his own projects. "You're passionate about it, and you're at the point in your career where you're ready and willing to get this film made. Go for it."

I sought advice from my uncle Chuck McCann, the Hollywood icon I'd looked up to since childhood. As an actor, comedian, puppeteer, and television personality, Chuck had seen every kind of story—and knew which ones worked.

"This is terrific. Three thumbs up," he said enthusiastically.

"Three thumbs?" I laughed, completely puzzled.

"Look," he said, leaning back and making a vintage Chuck face, "I believe with your dedication and storytelling abilities, this project will be better than two thumbs up."

We both laughed. That was Uncle Chuck—always knowing exactly how to motivate me with his signature humor.

"Have you thought about a title?"

Saved by Hannah, I said. "While we were trying for Hannah, I got diagnosed with cancer—which may have saved my life."

Chuck was quiet for a moment, then nodded slowly. "Perfect. That's your movie right there."

The filmmaker in me was finally ready to become the storyteller my family deserved—to tell how my cancer battle collided with Hannah's fight for life, and how, through it all, my wife Betsy and I realized we were soulmates for life.

My journey into storytelling began in 1986 with my first video camcorder and two toddlers. The moment I rolled tape with my new toy at Vasona Park in Los Gatos, I was hooked.

Soon, I was directing my three-year-old daughter, Hadley, in a short video for "The Late Show Starring Joan Rivers" contest—complete with a borrowed limo, professional makeup, and Hadley channeling Joan's signature attitude.

Hadley strutted with style. When the limo driver opened the door, I called cut and told Hadley to give him a high five and say, "You rock, Stanley," then get into the limo.

"You're a cool little kid," Stanley said after Hadley nailed it.

"Oh, grow up!" she retorted—exactly as I'd directed her to deliver that signature Joan comeback.

Stanley and I looked at each other and laughed like we were at a

Hollywood Comedy Show. It was an impressive first performance for my little pumpkin.

A couple of weeks later, I froze when I spotted "The Late Show" logo in our mailbox. Joan Rivers had written back! Her handwritten note invited Hadley and our family to be guests on an upcoming show. I couldn't believe our video had moved a comedy legend. That letter was validation that maybe I had what it took to be a real storyteller.

The reactions from friends and relatives after watching my early videos were unanimous: "You've missed your calling."

"I don't want to miss my calling," I told myself. I wasn't going to let this opportunity slip away.

Although the show was canceled before we could appear, that experience gave me the confidence to launch a career in independent film and video production. It was far from easy.

With three kids and a stay-at-home wife, I quit my job as a sales and marketing representative in late 1989 and got out of corporate America for good. It was the toughest decision I'd ever made, for obvious financial reasons. I prayed for guidance. However, not wanting to return to the corporate world fueled me to give everything I had—sometimes going overboard to secure gigs and ensure each project's success.

The first twenty professional jobs I filmed were weddings. I was frightened to death, pretending I knew what I was doing. I worked harder than ever, focused better than ever, and it paid off. Almost every client gave their video high praise.

I immediately realized the importance of networking. I made sure I was a team player and fun to work with. I'd exchange business cards with the photographer, catering person, and DJ, then follow up with thank-you notes with extra cards enclosed.

The networking paid off with referrals and dream clients—Google, eBay, the SF 49ers, Stanford University. I found myself working alongside Bay Area legends: Bill Walsh, Steve Wozniak, Peggy Fleming, John Elway, and the San Jose Sharks.

The more I filmed for clients, the more proficient in storytelling I became. For 28 years, I approached each of my 1,500 projects with one unwavering goal: to make it the best I'd ever created. Each project taught me something new about filmmaking and telling stories that mattered. I had no idea I was preparing for the most important story of my life, *Touched by Hannah*.

On April 13, 2013, my high school friend Deborah Howell reached out on Facebook. We'd reconnected through social media, and she'd been following my movie's progress.

"Hi Chris," she wrote. "You've been discussing titles for your film, and I see you've decided on *Saved by Hannah*. Well, this has been on my mind—my first waking thought this morning was *Touched by Hannah*."

Something clicked. I took a couple of days to think it over. *Saved by Hannah* had felt right. Going in for those tests because of Hannah led to my early cancer diagnosis. But "saved" carried assumptions I couldn't make with certainty.

Touched by Hannah was undeniably true. It took me back to those hours beside her incubator, my hand through that small opening, her tiny hand wrapped around my pointer finger. I was literally being touched by Hannah.

Touched by Hannah was it—moving forward, no other title even came close.

With the perfect title in place, I dove into writing the screenplay. But as pages accumulated, frustration set in. I realized I couldn't capture everything that mattered in a two-hour film. I made a decision that surprised even me—I shelved the movie and committed to writing the book first.

I wrote 110 pages in four months during the summer of 2013, but didn't finish the book until November 2024. Life interrupted in profound ways. When my dad died in 2016, it triggered severe depression and anxiety that left me unable to write for nearly three years.

Gravity felt quadrupled, making it hard to walk up the four steps onto my front porch. I was scared constantly, though nothing warranted fear. My positive, always-energetic self had vanished. At a party, when I tried my usual lightning-quick comeback—that typically made crowds erupt with laughter—nothing came. I couldn't access that part of me, and that was my identity.

The illness stole my ability to string words together, to think clearly, to access the creative mind I'd always relied on. My brain felt like it was shutting down, dying a little more each day. I didn't want to commit suicide—I had the best wife and kid on earth—but after several hundred days of this agony, I thought about ending the pain somehow.

I continued suffering greatly but somehow persevered and finally found the right psychiatrist and medication. Gradually, that horrible haze lifted from my brain, and I returned to life as usual—walking three miles a day and telling Hannah's story.

Before retiring from independent filmmaking, I'd submitted to film festivals for years with nothing to show for it. The most recognition I ever received was a ribbon from our local video group. But the disappointment never derailed me. I continued to refine my work, juggling multiple projects and learning from every video I produced. My clients consistently praised what I delivered, and I grew stronger as a filmmaker with each new project.

After retiring from professional filmmaking in 2018 and moving from San Jose to Woodland, California, I created *Yolo YoYo's,* a TV show that consumed all my creative energy for two years. Hannah's story would have to wait.

Season One became a local hit, and Season Two was even better. Our premiere episode, *Miracles on College Street*—an eleven-minute documentary I produced to promote *Touched by Hannah*—won awards coast to coast, including the "Film Heals" award at the 2022 Manhattan Film Festival (NYC) and runner-up for "Best Episode

West Coast" at the 2022 ACM Western Region WAVE Cable TV Awards in San Jose.

Receiving that kind of recognition for the first time was intoxicating and transformative.

After writing those first 110 pages of *Touched by Hannah*, I rewrote the manuscript twelve times, with each revision substantially improving it. Each of those twelve rewrites was supposed to be the last. I kept rewriting, grinding, learning, and refining until, by autumn 2023, I knew I'd taken it as far as I could alone. I needed professional help—it was finally time.

My author friend, Pete Cruz, mentioned my name to Cecil "Cec" Murphey, a New York Times bestselling author with 25 million books sold. "No room for another protégé," Cec said. My heart sank. Then: "But send me your first five pages."

Cec was a legend. One hundred dollars a month to his foundation. While other editors demanded thousands. Working with Cec was like an aspiring filmmaker working with Quentin Tarantino.

I sent my pages expecting nothing. I'd contacted other editors, but none could match Cec's reputation and affordable foundation fee.

His email arrived. I braced for rejection, ready to surrender my precious manuscript to strangers' hands.

Instead, Cec's words launched me into orbit: "You've hooked me on the first five pages. It's one of the best pieces I've received from a prospective protégé."

Twenty months of his old-school writer's boot camp transformed me into the writer Hannah's story deserved.

That validation carried me through every remaining page until the book was complete —the book Hannah deserved, the book our family's story demanded, the book that would finally give voice to those fragile, sacred moments when hope lived in the space between a giant finger and a micro-preemie's determined grasp.

Chris Hennessy
Filmmaker, Speaker, Author
chrishennessyfilms@gmail.com
https://www.henchris.com/
https://hennschtick.substack.com/

1

MY SOFT-TOUCH BABY AND I: MEDICAL MIRACLES REQUIRED

September 1, 2009

I hobbled from the parking lot, across the street from the Stanford Cancer Center, to see my surgeon, Doctor Peterkin. The unprecedented pain in my right ankle had started three days post radical prostatectomy on August 3, 2009. I remained resilient. I did my pre-surgery research and was aware of the 3 percent chance of developing life-threatening blood clots. *It's probably an infection*, I thought, not wanting to dwell on the worst-case scenario.

Since Doctor Peterkin had allowed me to resume walking two weeks after surgery, I chose not to share the issue—not even with my wife. I needed movement badly, ignored the foot discomfort, and hiked up to three miles daily.

I checked the building registry for Doctor Peterkin's suite number. *How neat that his office is across the street from the hospital.*

My uninjured but swollen, purple right ankle and the eight-inch-long wound below my belly button weren't my only problems. Betsy, my pregnant wife, called. "The doctor wants me to meet him at the hospital."

"The hospital? That's unexpected."

Betsy and I eagerly awaited the arrival of our daughter, Hannah, due on December 7, 2009. She had just started showing a couple of days earlier. When I noticed Betsy's growing belly, I exclaimed, "Hannah! That's our baby beneath those comfortable maternity clothes you shopped for with Mom."

The anticipation of Hannah's birth, a moment we had been dreaming of since our first date, gave us overwhelming joy and excitement. The memories of that special day, filled with warmth and nostalgia, still make us smile.

November 22, 1999

After meeting Betsy at the coffee and juice bar at Whole Foods the week before, and her mentioning that she was into power walking, I knew the Los Alamitos Creek Trail would be perfect for our first date. As we walked, I couldn't help but admire the beauty of the path that starts at Lake Almaden and runs along the creek.

I'd trekked this trail hundreds of times—dreamed of making movies, composed and practiced speeches, and thought about how I could enhance my kids' lives. I often took a few seconds to stop and rub random licorice root plants and delight in the delicious scent of pure, natural licorice on my fingers. After crossing the bridge, one and a half miles from the lake, I'd stretch for a couple of minutes on the ledge overlooking the flowing stream surrounded by trees, then reverse my direction over the bridge and head back to the lake.

"How did you get into walking and running?" I asked Betsy midway through our initial hike.

"I was burned out and quit volleyball after eleventh grade. I wanted to participate in an extracurricular activity, so I did when a friend asked me to try cross-country." She told me how much she enjoyed being outside and running with the comradery of her teammates. "I loved it. I also ran last year in junior college."

"Where did you go to high school, and what year did you graduate?" I asked nonchalantly.

"Davis High School, class of 1997." She paused and smirked. "You're asking my age."

"Wait a minute." I looked at my fingers and pretended to count. "I'm still trying to do the math."

"I'll turn twenty-two on May 9."

"You just want me to remember your birthday," I said, and we chuckled. "I'm forty-two." Our gaze remained connected as we both smiled.

"Enlighten me about Chris Hennessy."

"I'm a single parent to Hadley, fifteen, Harrison, thirteen, and Hendrix, eleven. My ex-wife and I were divorced in 1995. We have joint custody, but the kids are with me most of the time." I gave her some details and said, "When Hadley turned two, and Harrison was on the way, I was concerned because I didn't think it was possible to love another child like Hadley. But when he arrived, I loved him immediately and entirely."

"That's fantabulous. I babysat for the same two kids in Davis for several years from the time they were babies. It was a wondrous journey. I miss them."

"There's nothing like holding a baby. I miss that."

"Absolutely, me too. Do you ever think of having another?" Betsy asked.

"Another?"

"Another baby," she said.

Did I hear that correctly? "Um, yes, I've dreamed of having another little girl for years. What about you?"

"Of course. It's what girls dream of. First, one must find a perfect daddy." She smiled shyly.

"You never know when that guy will appear in Whole Foods and interrupt your study session."

"And energize the moment and the student."

We couldn't help staring into each other's eyes.

I'd made a list of what to look for in a future wife—no baggage or gossiping, cares for others, does not use alcohol or drugs, loves children and family, and is health conscious. Being a Christian was not on the list, but it soon became a real-deal bonus. *She seems to be everything I've dreamed of.*

The age difference was missing from my list. Earth has made too many orbits of the sun to count, and I've been here twenty-one more revolutions than Betsy. That pittance doesn't make me any better, wiser, or less eligible to be with her. Because I cared about the well-being of others and myself—I ate healthily, hydrated, exercised, slept well, and worked hard—most guessed I was ten or fifteen years younger. Age is really perception.

Betsy is more mature than I'll ever be. She liked me, and I liked her. We're two humans who connected and were smitten. I believed we should give it a shot—a testament to our deep connection and mutual understanding.

"It would be cool if she looked like Mommy," I said.

"I vote for a combination."

"Yes, I agree—if she has Mommy's eyes."

"Aw, really?"

"Definitely. Let's brainstorm names."

"Names? Oh . . . well, she'd have the best last name. Hennessy."

"You've got that right."

Betsy looked at me, then over to the creek, up to Mount Umunhum, and back to me. "Hannah Hennessy."

"Hannah Hennessy. I love it."

The name Hannah Hennessy immediately captivated our imaginations. Through the years, Hannah was the only name mentioned whenever we talked about having a child.

September 1, 2009

"Are you home?" I asked, my voice filled with concern for Betsy.

"Yes. It's probably not a big deal," Betsy said. "You see Doctor Peterkin, and I'll run errands after seeing Doctor Fisher."

"No, wait for me. I'm going with you. It'll allow us to look around the hospital and see where Hannah will be born." I called Doctor Peterkin's office to reschedule and headed home.

The trafficless drive had me parked in our driveway thirty-five minutes later. Betsy stood outside the front door, her face a mix of worry and discomfort. "Bets, how are you?" I asked, feeling the weight of the situation on my shoulders.

"I'm having severe stomach pain on and off."

"I'm sorry, baby. Let's go inside." I opened the door for her, and we walked into the kitchen. Then I hugged her gently and lightly massaged her neck, reassuring her. "Everything will be fine."

They may have left a couple of gallstones behind post-surgery three years ago. "Bets, I'll craft a stack of your favorite multi-grain pancakes if you still need to eat. Are you hungry?"

"You read my mind. I haven't eaten since yesterday's dinner. I'm famished."

As she nodded, the sun rays sneaking through the kitchen window perfectly backlit her curly, blonde-streaked hair. I had to caress that gorgeous little head.

"Tell me about last night's pregnancy yoga class," I said, then went to the counter and began mixing the pancake batter.

"I'm glad you asked. All the girls had back issues, morning sickness, tiredness, or weight gain. I was the only one without problems. I was grateful and happy for Hannah."

"I'm so proud of you, Bets. That's awesome!" We high-fived, and then I flipped the stack of pancakes onto a plate, handed it to her, and sat down. I looked into her seductive blue eyes as she devoured breakfast.

"When did the stomach pain begin?"

"I felt uncomfortable pressure in my stomach when we lay down last night. I eventually went to the bathroom and noticed spotting."

"I wish you would have said something."

"I didn't want to worry you. I called the advice line and was told that pressure and spotting were normal during pregnancy. Before long, it turned into severe pain that lasted a couple of minutes and then went away. It continually came back and then dissipated."

"I can't believe I slept through that."

"You've been through so much, Chris. Sleeping helps heal. I didn't think it was necessary to wake you."

"No problem. When did you speak to the doctor?"

"After you left this morning, I got out of bed and had to lie back down. I called the doctor, and he told me to meet him at the hospital."

She grabbed her stomach and winced. I stood behind her, scratched her back, and whispered, "Father God, please watch over Betsy and Hannah." In two minutes, the piercing pain dissipated.

My mind functions better when I move, so I went to the sink and washed the dishes. *Maybe it was something she ate, a yoga stretch gone awry, or the gallstones.* I was oblivious and confused.

"Did you guys do yoga or just sit around the circle chatting?"

"Oh yes, we did, baby. We learned the downward dog pose, the most simple, effective stretch ever. My hamstrings, calves, Achilles, neck, and back feel loose. I wish I had known this when I ran cross-country in college."

"You're going to have to show me," I said.

"Absolutely. When we get home from the doctor before our walk."

"Perfect."

"Yoga should be a protocol for pregnant women."

I nodded.

"Chris, please find the Lamaze flyer and sign us up for classes before we leave. I'm going to the bedroom to get ready."

"You just began week twenty-six of pregnancy. I read we're not supposed to start Lamaze until week thirty-two. That's mid-October."

"Honey, if you want to be there coaching me through our daughter's birth, Lamaze is crucial. Please sign us up today."

"You got it, girl." I gave a thumbs-up, filled out the form, and met Betsy in our bedroom.

"Will you please change that hideous shirt? You wore it yesterday."

I held my breath, slid the shirt over my head, and threw it in the dirty clothes hamper.

"Chris, please get that shirt out of the bedroom before I throw up."

I stuck my tongue out, wiggled it at her, smiled, and grabbed my favorite T-shirt. Puckering my lips, I blew a kiss, then turned, headed for the washroom, and tossed the shirt in the washing machine before returning to the bedroom. "Are you ready, baby?"

"Yup."

I took Betsy's left arm as I did after the officiant pronounced us husband and wife. "Queen Betsy, may I escort you to the car?"

She smiled. I led the way to the front door, opened it, and guided us down the steps.

Our neighbor Ali waved. "Where are you guys off to?"

"Paradise," I yelled back. That was our usual response to each other when leaving the house with no vital destination.

I stepped off the curb onto the street, and my foot buckled. "Ow!" I cried out. Betsy looked my way, and I forced a smile. I didn't understand why my foot was inflamed and hurting. It wasn't injured in a fall or accident. It just started bothering me in the hospital—a couple of days after surgery.

"Are you okay?" Betsy asked.

I must be okay right now for Betsy. "I'm good. Let's do this." I ignored the pain and focused on driving.

I gingerly placed my aching foot on the gas pedal, and we began an unhurried drive to the hospital. Twelve minutes later, we pulled into the parking lot.

As I opened the car door, I inhaled the familiar aroma of freshly crushed garlic carried by the crisp summer morning sea breeze from nearby Gilroy, the world's garlic capital. The smell drifts into South San José during harvest—from late June through early September—and an all-day, cooling sea breeze always follows when the delicious odor persists past 9 a.m.

We grasped hands and walked to the main entrance. I held the door for Betsy and followed her inside.

"May I help you?" The candy striper at the welcome desk could see we had no idea where to go.

"We're looking for Labor and Delivery," I said.

"Walk straight down the hall." She pointed in that direction. "You'll see the elevators. Get off on the second floor."

"Thanks so much."

We arrived at the elevator. After waiting several seconds, the doors opened, and a couple came out holding their baby.

"Are you guys leaving?" I asked.

"Yes. Jaylen is two days old. Taking him home is incredible."

"Gorgeous," Betsy said.

And I followed up with, "Good luck."

"Thank you," the mom said, and they walked off to live happily ever after.

"That's going to be us in a few months," I told Betsy as I held the elevator door open for her.

We exited on the second floor. The sign on the left read NICU. I had yet to learn what that meant. We went right and headed into the labor and delivery area.

Looking at our surroundings, I said, "Three months from now, this is where Hannah will be born." Betsy walked with her head down, obviously in pain, and didn't acknowledge my comment. I took her hand and intertwined her fingers with mine.

We arrived at the reception area and approached the nurse at the counter. Betsy said, "I'm Betsy Hennessy. My doctor told me to meet him here."

"Yes, Mrs. Hennessy. Doctor Fisher told us to expect you." The nurse greeted us warmly. Her voice and body language projected a welcoming vibe, instantly putting us at ease.

Betsy started to fill out the required paperwork, but the nurse noticed she could barely hold a pen and stand. "Let's not worry about the paperwork. You need to be lying down." She turned to an assistant and said, "Molly, please take this couple to patient room 1A." She took the pen from Betsy, gently held her pointer finger, and smiled. "Everything is going to be just fine."

"Thank you," Betsy mumbled.

Molly guided us to room 1A. Instead of escorting Queen Betsy, I practically held her up.

"Let's put on this gown." Betsy undressed, and Molly helped her into the garment and the bed. She closed the cubicle curtain. "Your nurse will be here shortly. Please press the button if you need anything," she said and left.

"Why leave us behind a closed curtain in a small, dark area?" Betsy asked. "It's claustrophobic."

I opened the curtain, and an abundance of natural light immediately illuminated our area. "It feels bright and roomy now." Betsy looked comfortable under the soft hospital blanket.

A nurse arrived. "We need to do a couple of tests," she said confidently. Then she proceeded with a blood draw and gave Betsy a bottle to collect urine. "The results will be delivered in twenty to thirty minutes. Now, I'm going to give you a cervical exam."

She lifted Betsy's gown to do the examination, and within seconds her head arose. She looked at Betsy with panic-stricken eyes. "You're nine centimeters. I'm so sorry."

"What does that mean?" I asked.

"It means your baby is coming very soon. I need to alert the staff." She hurried out of the room to get help. The chilling sound of steps racing down the hallway echoed into our room.

Betsy grabbed me so hard that her fingernails dug into my arm. I didn't look, but it felt as if I had been knifed in my left bicep.

"She's not going to make it! She's not going to make it! I just read yesterday that her lungs have not yet developed. Hannah's going to die! God, help us!"

An adrenaline rush shifted my mood from relaxed and clueless to fight or flight. There was no written protocol for what to do or how to react in such a situation, and I didn't have the luxury of time to think it out. *I must comfort Betsy.*

I took her hand, examined her beautiful, horror-filled eyes, and presented my first-ever motivational speech, 100 percent ad-lib.

"With teamwork, prayer, patience, and love, we'll make it through this," I said with conviction. "I have no doubts Hannah will be a strong, healthy, beautiful girl like her mom. She will have a long, extraordinary life with the best mother and father. We're going to accomplish a wonderful life together."

"With you by my side, I can do anything."

I took her soft, angelic face into my hands. "I have complete faith in Betsy Walter Hennessy. Father God will be holding our hands, always."

Betsy settled down, but Hannah was coming, and nothing could be done about it. Nature was taking its course.

NICU professionals quickly assembled in our room, which appeared to be a mini version of rush hour in Silicon Valley.

We both listened as Doctor Powers, the Director of NICU, explained the situation and statistics. "Betsy is going to deliver Hannah very soon, and you're in for a long fight. Here's what you're up against. A baby born as early as Hannah is likely to suffer short-term and long-term health problems. In the long term, Hannah may develop cerebral palsy and struggle with impaired cognitive ability, which can lead to learning disabilities, vision problems, dental issues, and behavioral and psychological problems. There's an increased risk of SIDS.

"If Hannah survives the first few weeks, then the short-term complications—"

I quit paying attention. Surviving was just the start, and that was our immediate priority.

A nurse asked me to step out for a couple of minutes while they prepared Betsy. I left for the restroom.

As I walked to the men's room, my mind flashed back eight months earlier when the roles had been reversed.

"Mr. Hennessy, your PSA level has nearly doubled to 18.7. This indicates prostate cancer," Doctor Jack explained. "Your sperm levels are quite low. The chances are not favorable for conceiving a child. I'm so sorry. The next step is a prostate biopsy next week. I know you're trying to make a baby, but after the biopsy, conceiving will not be possible."

Our hearts sank. Tears slid down the nurse's cheek.

"Wait, Doctor Jack," I fired back. "We want to try another month or two for Hannah." I looked at Betsy, knowing God helped me spit those words out.

When I returned to the room, Betsy was gone, but a nurse stayed behind and helped me don a medical outfit. "Mr. Hennessy, please follow me. Betsy is in the delivery room."

We walked into the hall, took a left, and headed to Betsy's and my destiny.

"See the people surrounding that incubator?" The nurse stopped, turned to the room on the right, and pointed. "They're waiting for Hannah."

Six medical professionals were in a closed-off-from-the-world room, standing around an empty incubator.

We walked another twenty feet and turned left into the delivery room, where another team prepared for Hannah. I was impressed that the NICU team for Hannah had been assembled so quickly and efficiently.

Betsy was lying down, noticeably in pain. A NICU nurse held her left hand and offered encouragement while the respiratory therapist checked oxygen levels.

"Mr. Hennessy, I'm Doctor Maddy, the NICU obstetrician specialist." She looked into my eyes and firmly shook my hand. "I'll be delivering Hannah. After she arrives, we'll prepare her to enter her incubator."

She was poised and probably had delivered a thousand NICU babies. *We're in good hands.*

I prayed and cried while the NICU nurse did Lamaze coaching. She told Betsy to push like she was constipated. Betsy looked at me, her face distressed. I took her free hand and, in her ear, gently said, "I love you, and I'm here for you. You're doing great."

I bowed my head over Betsy and prayed. "Father God, please offer your astonishing strength to care for Betsy and Hannah. Please help them get through this alive, with their health intact." I was worried about Betsy and terrified for Hannah, and I braced myself for the unknown outcome.

A few minutes later, Hannah popped out right into the hands of the obstetrician specialist. Betsy told me later that she never saw it happen. "I didn't stress about seeing Hannah at that time. I just wanted her to get the care she needed."

I counted limbs, fingers, and toes. Normal. She was gorgeous, and I loved her instantly, just as I did her three siblings, who had been born more than twenty years earlier. I was again going to be the most dedicated dad around.

Hannah weighed a mere 1 lb., 9 oz.—about the same weight as a quart of milk—and was classified as a micropreemie. I'd never seen anything like it, heard the word preemie, or known that not all hospitals had a Neonatal Intensive Care Unit (NICU). Now, I had the micro version of a preemie, and the NICU was going to be Hannah's first, and hopefully not her only, home.

The doctor worked quickly and effortlessly before handing Hannah to the respiratory therapist. Instead of being placed gently into her mother's loving arms, Hannah was placed into her new home, an incubator, and the therapist whisked her into the room across the hall.

Betsy was breathing like she had just run a 5K road race. Moist makeup rolled down her cheeks, and her tangled hair partially covered that naturally gorgeous, sweaty face. Her head was motionless, and her eyes were wide open, probably not seeing anything.

"Betsy," I said, but she didn't acknowledge me. She had the look of *What the heck just happened?* on her face.

A nurse arrived. "It's time to take Betsy to her room." She helped Betsy stand and guided her into a wheelchair because she was in no condition to walk. The nurse wheeled her into the elevator, her room, and then into bed. Hannah's mommy soon fell asleep. I tiptoed out of the room and headed downstairs to see Hannah.

I entered the NICU for the first time. Hannah's incubator was the second on the right. Tubes and wires were everywhere, including in her mouth and nose. She had bandages and splints on her legs and arms, and a CPAP mask covered her face.

Doctor Powers approached. "Mr. Hennessy, Hannah is fighting for her life." Nothing has ever hit me as hard as hearing that one horrible sentence. Those words ripped through my shirt, slit my chest open, and seized what was left of my heart.

"We were able to take her off the ventilator. She's got a good pair of lungs. That's her first mountain conquered. There's still an entire range to scale. Next, we need to get her digestive system moving."

I looked at one-pound-nine-ounce Hannah. *Could that tiny body even have a digestive system?*

The doctor offered the most vital advice we received throughout our ordeal. "As great as technology is, what is best for Hannah right now is Mommy and Daddy's touch, voice, and scent."

I completely understood.

The only physical contact possible with Hannah was sticking an arm through a small hole into the side of the incubator. When my huge pointer finger brushed Hannah's micro-tiny hand, she grabbed it and held on, and we stayed connected for up to several hours at a time.

I sang ad-lib songs and prayers while bonding with my baby three months before we were supposed to. When she wrapped her tiny fingers around mine, they felt as soft as snowflakes falling unhurriedly from a silent, stormy sky, landing gently on my finger.

I thought up a song that became my anthem to Hannah. I repeatedly crooned, "Hann's a soft-touch baby, like outbreaks of snowflakes floating onto Hannah and me. My heart has defrosted. I'm here for you always, my soft-touch baby."

Whenever I was with my soft-touch baby, I was truly in the moment.

Both of us faced a long, daunting road ahead. The odds were that one or both of us wouldn't make it. Tomorrow was a frightening thought. However, when living in the moment, there wasn't a tomorrow. And when tomorrow doesn't exist, there's no stressing about it. I felt honored, blessed, and cherished every second I sat there, touched by Hannah.

2

MY WORST FIRST LINE EVER

I was a single dad with three kids. My in-home office enabled me to spend more time with my children than most dads. Someone had told me, "Nobody has ever regretted spending too much time with their kids." I certainly didn't. I embraced those fleeting moments.

One day, while motoring my son Harrison and his buddy Ryan from basketball practice, we stopped to shop at Whole Foods Market. The boys stayed in the car, talking hoops and listening to their hip-hop radio music.

Because I was a shop-without-a-list shopper, I sped through every aisle with my cart—my eyes scouring the shelves like a speed reader. I quickly snatched what we needed to survive for the next few days.

As I hurried through the juice and coffee bar to the exit, the evening's schedule preoccupied my mind. *How long will driving home, preparing dinner, and getting Hendrix to basketball practice take*? I did the math. Timewise, I was good. And then I spotted a gorgeous gal sitting and reading. Our eyes met. *Look at those Caribbean-blue eyes.* We each turned away. As I passed, our eyes met again—a classic double take.

The next move changed my life. Instinct took over. I walked one step past her, then abruptly halted. I shifted into reverse, like a NASCAR driver, and pulled my cart back so I could see those eyes. If my groceries weren't protected in the enclosed cart, they'd have scattered all over the floor.

I usually can improvise an attention-grabbing first line. This time I choked. "You remind me of an ex-girlfriend." That was hands-down my worst first line ever.

The courage to approach her and say something was more critical than my first words. Now, I had to think about damage control. Like an actor messing up lines during a theatrical performance, I proceeded as if nothing had gone awry.

"Hello, I'm Chris."

"Hey, Chris," she said with a broad smile. "I'm Betsy." She reached out her right hand and gave a firm handshake.

An avalanche of well-spoken sentences flowed naturally and effortlessly, directly from my heart, out of my mouth, and into her ears.

"Betsy, I'm having a premonition." I put my hand on the side of my head and closed my eyes, appearing to be in deep thought. I'd already seen her science book and glanced at the San José State notebook. "Hmm. You're a student." I paused. "You're a student at San José State, studying science."

"Very good," Betsy said. "I'm studying for a big test on Monday."

She appeared fit and healthy, and health-minded folks hung out at Whole Foods. "You're also into working out and healthy living."

"You got that right. I enjoy walking, running, and eating healthy. I listen to country music, love my family, and play sports."

"That's awesome, Betsy. Same here." I put my hand back on my head. "Another incoming premonition." With closed eyes, my entire face squinted. "You're going to make an 'A' on your test."

"Your intuition is amazing," she said, laughing. "The encouragement is welcome."

"There's a final premonition. Wow, this is a good one."

"Tell me."

"You and I will soon meet up on my favorite trail for a three-mile hike," I said, and we chuckled.

"My sixth sense tells me that would be a fun time." She picked up her pen and ripped a small sheet of paper from her spiral notebook.

As Betsy jotted down her phone number, I saw Harrison and Ryan peeking through the glass door, probably wondering why it was taking so long. They witnessed Betsy hand me that invaluable piece of paper. Harrison turned, Ryan gave me a thumbs-up, and they returned to the car.

I called Betsy on Monday evening. "How did you do on the test?"

"Studying at Whole Foods, there were distractions. They must have helped because I aced it."

"Way to go," I said and applauded. "Let's celebrate on the trail. Can you meet up tomorrow at about 6 p.m.?"

"That works. I totally look forward to it."

Tuesday, November 16, 1999

I shaved for the first time all week, put on jeans and a T-shirt, walked into the kitchen, grabbed a coffee, entered the dining room and through the living room, and stepped into my office.

Besides working from home, my favorite fringe benefit of being a sole proprietor was that I could wear whatever and shave whenever. I worked hard, mostly doing two people's jobs. I also enjoyed having a life outside of work and regularly took advantage of exercise, a round of golf during the week, and bonding with my kids while coaching their sports teams. This balance between work and personal life was crucial, especially as a single dad.

I'd written, produced, and directed dozens of professional videos for organizations such as Google, OfficeMax, eBay, and the San Francisco 49ers, as well as hundreds of weddings and bar mitzvahs. Persistence, consistency, dedication, enjoyment, and hard work made me a confident, polished filmmaker.

Tuesday was a typical, busy day. I edited a video, consulted with clients, answered emails, and returned phone calls. I looked forward to finishing work and getting outside on the trail.

At 5:45 p.m., I left the house, cruised by Almaden Lake, and entered the park. In gorgeous weather, I sat at a picnic table overlooking Almaden Lake on one side and the parking lot on the other. I planned to take Betsy on the creek path, secluded between the rippling creek on one side and the grassy hills on the other.

At 6:15 p.m., I wasn't the slightest bit rattled. *She's probably stuck in traffic,* I reassured myself. I stood, walked over to the bocce courts, stretched my hamstrings on the bench, and returned to the picnic table. At 6:30 p.m., I left for a necessary, lonely three-mile walk. *She stood me up!* I would have bet money that she'd show. As I walked, I couldn't help but wonder what might have happened. *Did she forget? Was there an emergency? Or did she simply change her mind?*

Dejected and overcome with frustration, I walked three miles near my record pace. *An issue regarding school likely came up. I hope she's okay.* I was bummed, but exercising had me uplifted and hopeful.

I went home, and we'd just finished dinner when the home phone rang. "I'm so sorry," Betsy said. "I left my place without directions. When I got home, it was too late to drive back." She didn't own a cellphone.

"No problem." *She hadn't purposely blown me off!* "I figured something had come up. Why don't you come over and enjoy leftovers from last night's leftovers?"

"Thanks, Chris." She chuckled. "I'll pass, but I'd love to reschedule."

"How about next Monday, 5:30 p.m.?"

"Perfect."

"I'll see you then."

I hung up and hollered up the stairs. "Harrison and Hendrix. Get down here, clear the table, and wash the dishes." They responded with laughter. I turned around and saw an immaculate kitchen. "Thanks, guys!" I twisted the music volume control louder and danced around the living room, delighted.

Monday, November 22, 1999

As soon as I got in the car, my adrenaline started flowing. We finally met up at the trail.

"Putting the directions in my car last night worked," Betsy said.

"Great. I'm happy to see you."

"Do you like my new walking shoes?"

"New Balance. That's a good shoe. I love the color."

"Thanks. They're also comfortable and supportive."

As we walked, we conversed about all sorts of things, including the endorphins streaming through my system. "You know, those are produced by our God-given brains, the most amazing part of our organisms, which are tasked with controlling our nervous system. Such greatness had to be manufactured by God," she said. "It's too remarkable to have happened by chance." She brought up lots of other things that caused me to ponder.

I wasn't aware whether I believed until Betsy made God seem as real as the myriad of stars seen from our breathtaking Sierra Nevada Mountains. I'd never again consider that everything happened by some cosmic crapshoot.

"Let's head to the creek," I said.

Nothing is more conducive to first-date conversation than being outside and moving through the cool sea breezes, combined with just enough of a feeling that we were away from it all. We finished a comfortably paced three-mile walk and gulped water from the same two-liter bottle Betsy had brought.

"Betsy, look up." We stood under three majestic redwood trees.

"That's the most gorgeous sight ever."

"Have you ever walked three miles on a date?" I asked.

"I've never dated a guy who walked or ran."

"Well, you have now."

For the next hour, we frequently gazed into each other's eyes, clowned around, and chatted about family, friends, and other topics that arose—including having a baby named Hannah Hennessy.

"Tell me about your relationship with the kids," Betsy said.

"I recently finished coaching Harrison and Hendrix junior high cross-country team for the fifth straight season. When I started, twelve kids came out to practice. This past season, we had about ninety per practice."

"How did you manage that?" She seemed genuinely interested in hearing me out.

"My strategy was simple. I'd have them run just long enough so they wouldn't quit. Those who finished practice got a fruit squeeze ice pop."

"Very clever."

"The other coaches heard about the one hundred multicolored ice pops for five dollars at Costco and copycatted me."

"That's hilarious. You've led kids to run and enhanced their lives. I'm proud of you, Chris. What do you enjoy most about coaching?"

"I enjoy being with Harrison and Hendrix during an extracurricular activity and communicating with all the kids. I delight in encouraging and making them laugh while providing inspiration with short, uplifting improv speeches. So far, it's worked." Eager to learn more about her, I said, "Your turn. Tell me about Betsy."

"My dad was a Christian youth leader at Young Life for seventeen years. He's currently in outside sales. My mom is a grade school teacher. Her temperament is perfect—the students and families love her.

"When I was sixteen, my dad bought a small truck for us to share. Soon, that truck was just mine. I think that was his plan," she said, cracking up. "I had a phone in my room. My brothers didn't. Maybe that's why my brother Joe doesn't speak to me." She laughed. "I'm totally kidding."

"Are you close to Joe?"

"Yes, I have good relationships with my three siblings, Steve, Tim, and Joe. They're each like Dad in different ways."

"Tell me more about your dad."

"Dad reminds us of Ben Cartwright from TV's *Bonanza*—the patriarch and rock, a hardworking man who always puts family first. Dad is a Division II College Hall of Fame linebacker from Lewis and Clark. He's always had an inexhaustible 'I can and will do this' approach when faced with big jobs and tough tasks. My friends and family say I'm a lot like him."

Betsy impressed me with the way she conducted herself during the conversation. I'd done business with hundreds of clients, including famous Silicon Valley executives, well-known sports celebrities, and radio and TV personalities. Her voice projection, assertiveness, and ability to articulate were as good as any. "What activities did your parents guide you into?"

"Every summer, my brothers and I got to go on Dad's youth group trips to Woodleaf Young Life Camp. I met many of my friends there. It was a crucial, safe extracurricular. The leaders were mentors who helped grow my faith and role models I could go to when needed. Hanging out in the circle around a campfire, talking, singing, being real, no cliques or judgment, just total support. It was a blessing for me."

"Being exposed to youth group sounds like a glorious gift for any child."

"I must give the credit to Mom and Dad. I'm very thankful."

"Many children don't have loving and supportive families. You're a lucky woman."

"I totally agree."

"How did you get into film and video?"

"I purchased my first video camera in 1986 to film the kids and was immediately drawn to telling stories via video. Several friends said I'd missed my calling. Their comments and my love for story-telling via video motivated me to research the relatively new field of videography. I quit my job as a sales and marketing representative in 1990, and without taking a film or video class, I became a full-time, independent video producer."

"That's awesome. You're dedicated and pursuing your passion."

"Exactly. I can accomplish more than weddings, events, and

corporate videos. However, being with the kids is more important than following my dreams."

"Your kids are fortunate to have a dad who wants to spend time with them."

I smiled and said, "Thank you. Tell me about your studies."

"This is my first year at San José State studying dietetics, which focuses on the interaction between nutrition and health."

"What do you hope to do with a dietetics degree?"

"I'd like to work in healthcare, supervising food service and patient nutritional needs. My dream is to eventually provide medical nutrition therapy to patients with various health concerns, especially diabetes."

A hummingbird zoomed up to our faces and hovered, flew backward to Betsy, forward to me, and accelerated extraordinarily fast to the lake.

We found ourselves in a picturesque scene, surrounded by wild blackberry plants—heavy with juicy, black, clustered berries—and red willow trees, their lengthy, graceful branches leaning earthward toward the babbling creek, spilling into the lake. The beauty of nature seemed to amplify our emotions.

I couldn't resist pulling Betsy close. We embraced and then kissed. An hour of pure joy passed in what might have been the most prolonged public display of affection on that trail. Our happiness radiated from us like a beacon.

We temporarily became part of the landscape I'd traversed a thousand times. The sunny skies had turned overcast, but we didn't notice. A steady rain began to fall, and we didn't care. We focused only on each other. Gene Kelly could have been dancing and singing in the rain. The presidential motorcade may have passed by, and maybe it did, but we missed it.

Although I wanted to linger longer in the sweetness of her lips, our mouths finally separated, and we began to breathe our own air again.

Betsy pounded her foot into a puddle and giggled. "We're drenched."

The moderate rainfall turned heavy. "It feels like we're showering with our clothes on."

"It's wonderful!" Betsy said.

"That was a fabulous walk and talk. Splish, splash, we're taking a bath," I sang out, then hammered the puddle with my right foot. "A toast to many more trail walks."

"Absolutely," Betsy said as raindrops slid off her sunny smile.

This was love at first walk.

Betsy closed her eyes, smiled, and rested her head on my chest. We walked, arm in arm, through our puddle-filled, sloppy trail to the parking lot, floating off the ground together.

3

KETCHUP SONGS AND DREAMS OF A BABY HANNAH

December 10, 1999

In the early evening of Friday, December 10, Betsy and I hung out in the kitchen after a three-mile hike on the trail. "Can you explain hydration?" I asked as she stood at the sink, rapidly and delicately dissecting a grapefruit.

"Hydration means replacing fluids lost through sweating and eliminating waste. Every cell, tissue, and organ in our body needs water to work properly."

"Hydration is our friend," I said, then asked, "What is dehydration?"

"Dehydration is a bad word. Your blood becomes more concentrated, making your cardiovascular system work harder to efficiently pump blood. Waste accumulates and damages the kidneys. Everything is affected, including energy level, mood, and well-being."

"Thank you for inspiring me to hydrate," I said, walking to the sink. The strainer was full of rindless, segmented grapefruit pieces. I ate one and then another. "These are better than candy."

"And much healthier."

The two of us sat at the kitchen table and devoured all the sweet, juicy, tart, delicious, and easy-to-eat pieces of fruit in two minutes. Her grapefruit routine became part of our after-walk hydration ritual.

Betsy mentioned she might meet up with school friends and attend a party. My sons were at their mom's place, and I didn't want to be alone. I wanted to be with Betsy.

"Chris, I need to call Lisa about the party," she said. "May I call from your home phone?"

"Sure," I said. Our landline was located next to the kitchen table. I entered the living room and turned the music on to avoid listening to their conversation.

After a minute, she walked into the living room. "I told Lisa I wouldn't be able to make it."

She wants to be with me! I suggested Giorgio's, my favorite Italian restaurant. "Let's celebrate Friday night with the best pizza and pasta dishes in San José."

"That sounds terrific."

We left the house just as my daughter, Hadley, arrived. As she exited her car, I smiled and said, "Hadey, I didn't expect to see you."

"Hey, Dad, I'm running behind and must rush inside to grab a few things."

"Got it. Hadley, this is Betsy. Betsy, this is my little pumpkin, Hadley."

"It's great to meet you, Betsy," Hadley said, and they shook hands and looked into each other's eyes. "The boys and I have heard so much about you."

"Your dad has told me about your running," Betsy answered. "I'm hoping to see an upcoming race."

"That would be great. I look forward to chatting again."

"Me too, Hadley."

Hadley hurried into the house, and we got into Betsy's car.

"Chris, she's beautiful and looks like an elite runner," Betsy said. She shifted into drive, and we headed off to Giorgio's.

"Thanks. Hopefully, the three of us can get together soon," I said as we passed Dartmouth Middle School. "That's where the boys go to school. There's the field where I've coached too many cross-country practices to count."

Two and three-tenths of a mile later, we turned into the Giorgio's parking area. "That's a delicious Italian aroma," Betsy said as we exited the car.

"South Bay's best." I took her hand, and we walked to the restaurant. "It reminds me of Mom's Sunday night homemade smorgasbords—chicken cutlets, eggplant parmigiana, prime rib meatballs, and pasta with sauce made from scratch."

We entered a lively atmosphere featuring Italian music, a spirited crowd buzz, the happily hustling staff sporting black pants and red Giorgio's polo shirts, and dim lighting with a soft, romantic orange glow.

The hostess sat us face-to-face in a cozy booth for two with cushioned seats, ideally situated in the back corner. We each looked at a menu.

"Fresh agua," the busboy said, filling our glasses with filtered water.

"Let's share the spinach salad," Betsy suggested.

"We could also share their veggie chicken pasta dish."

Betsy raised her glass. "A toast to a delicious, healthy meal."

I lifted mine as well. "And to hydrating and enjoying a well-deserved, relaxing Friday night."

We clinked glasses and gulped our water.

"Bets, is an occasional Diet Pepsi okay?" That was the first time I called her Bets.

"I love an occasional Diet Pepsi, especially with Italian food," she said. "Let's go for it."

The waitress took our order, and then Betsy asked me, "Have you ever thumb-wrestled?"

"Yes," I answered, "and I've never lost."

When members of the opposite sex engage in a thumb war, it's not about winning or losing. It's about your hooked fingers touching while your thumbs caress playfully—flirtatious maximus.

We began the first of many affectionate thumb-wrestling contests.

We talked, we wrestled, and casually ate fine Italian food.

"How is school?" I asked.

"I'll have to focus on studying this weekend. Finals are next week. I'm looking forward to December 15, the first day of Christmas break."

"How long until you go back?"

"January 10. You and I have many trail walks to accomplish before then. Friends from school say the Christmas in the Park display in downtown San José is a must-see."

"The kids and I have visited every year since they were toddlers. We'll head over there after finals."

She grabbed my thumb with hers and trapped it, holding it down. "One, two, three, four, I declare a thumb war." She let go of my hand. "I win!"

Thumb wrestling while chatting became regular Giorgio's foreplay. Others sitting nearby might have thought we were crazy—and we were crazy—about each other.

The waitress came over and asked, "How was everything?"

"Delicious!" I touched the tips of my fingers and thumb to my lips, kissed them lightly, and thrust them into the air.

"Grazie," she said while nodding. "May I ask who won the thumb game?"

"I let her win." The three of us chuckled.

Betsy chimed in. "Holding hands for twenty minutes was a win-win."

"Congratulazioni," the waitress said, looking at us. "I knew that you both won."

"May we ask your name?"

"Vittoria."

"Vittoria, I'm Chris, and this is Betsy. We're very pleased to meet you."

"You've been great," Betsy said.

"Chris and Betsy, it's lovely to meet you. Finito?" Vittoria smiled.

"We're finished. Right, Betsy?"

"I'm good until tomorrow's breakfast," Betsy said.

"That makes me muy contenta," Vittoria said, handing me the

bill. She grabbed the dirty plates, cutlery, and my credit card. "I'll be right back."

She returned quickly and left the receipt. "Chris and Betsy, please come back soon."

"We will definitely see you soon, Vittoria," Betsy said.

As we walked to her car, Betsy commented about our experience. "Giorgio's is my new favorite eatery. Thank you so much for a fabulous meal."

"You're very welcome. Everything was great, except for—"

"Except for?" Betsy asked.

"Except for losing our thumb war. I can't wait for the rematch."

"That's an excellent excuse for another hand-caressing date, Mr. Hennessy."

"Exactly," I said, gently touching her shoulder. "Let's stop at Lucky's Market and grab a few things."

We found parking, grabbed a small carry basket on our way inside, and filled it with three boxes of sugarless cereal, two cartons of soy milk, four protein bars, one bunch of bananas, six apples, two grapefruits, and one bottle of ketchup.

"Are you buying one bottle of ketchup on a two-for-one night?" the checker asked.

"I'm sorry," I said, chuckling and wondering if I'd heard him correctly.

"Are you buying one bottle of ketchup on a two-for-one night, sir?" he asked again, pointing to a promotional sign.

I laughed. "This one bottle of ketchup on a two-for-one night will last through next summer. I'm good."

"That's fine," the cashier said, scanning our groceries.

I started packing our items into the paper bag. A tune and words came, and I sang, "I bought one bottle of ketchup on a two-for-one night. There's no need to waste money on another tomato delight."

The people in the line behind us laughed. "That's a perfect first line for the hit country song I'm going to write and record." I repeated the verse. "I bought one bottle of ketchup on a two-for-one night. There's no need to waste money on another tomato delight."

I paid the bill, took our bag of groceries, and we sauntered off through the exit doors, singing my future chart-topping tune all the way to the back of the parking lot and into Betsy's car.

"Did you know girls dig handsome, confident guys?" Betsy asked when we were about to drive off. "You're organically funny, enjoy it, and laugh as much as your subjects." We turned onto Almaden Expressway. "I've never met anyone who could improvise a song on the spot and make everybody around, including me, laugh. It's the best gift you could give yourself."

We stopped at a red light, and I turned to Betsy and kissed her head. "Thank you for making me feel—"

"Look! Christmas trees!" Betsy shouted when she saw the Almaden Florist ahead on the right.

"Let's make a stop," I suggested.

Betsy drove slowly in the right lane, turned, and parked. I went to the driver's side and opened the door. "Let's head into Christmas."

Betsy bolted out of the car and took charge. I followed her through aisles of fresh, dark green, and slightly damp Christmas trees. She obviously wanted to look at every tree on the premises. She stopped and pointed when we reached the end of the last aisle. "This one." It was the second-to-last tree on the lot.

I chuckled, and we high-fived. "This is perfect. Definitely the best of the lot."

"You're coming with us," Betsy said to the tree.

I heaved the seven-foot Douglas fir onto my back and led Betsy to the cashier. Not being on a time schedule and sipping hot chocolate together on a cloudy, chilly December night inspired an early atmosphere of Christmas spirit.

I stopped, took the tree off my back, and held it beside me. "The boys are going to love it," I said, and then asked the cashier, "What would it take for us to be able to bring this tree home?"

"Did you just land from Saturn?" he asked.

"We're actually from Pluto, but we drive a Saturn." I turned and directed him to Betsy's white Saturn.

He looked over, then back, nodded, and pointed to the price tag while remaining expressionless.

"Do you guys take cash?" I asked. He nodded. I took a wad of cash from my pocket and deadpanned. "I'm so sorry." I paused and shook my head. "All I've got is exact change. Is that okay?"

He nodded again, straight-faced, and we completed the transaction.

I thought he was emotionless, like a robot, and then he blurted out, "Thanks for being the most hilarious customer I've ever served."

I whirled my wide-eyed face around to Betsy and then back to the cashier. "Next time, would you show your appreciation by laughing?" I asked, throwing my hands up and making it appear I was upset. "Earth is weird," I said and shook my head. "On Pluto, we laugh if something is funny."

His jolly, loud laughter projected spirited holiday merriment. He hugged Betsy and me, then turned to serve the next customer.

"Chris, you changed his attitude and made his night," Betsy said as I hurried through the exit before her, hauling a heavy load on my back.

"What a sweet thing to say. Thanks, Betsy." I tied the tree to the roof, closed her door, ensured the tree was appropriately secured to the top of the car, and entered on the passenger's side. "It's been a magical night. Let's chill out at the house."

"Maybe the magic has just begun?"

"Our lives have just begun, Betsy Walter." We took a left turn onto Almaden Expressway. Her Saturn's tires rolled across planet Earth's surface for two miles, and we pulled into my driveway.

I untied the tree, took it to the back gate, opened the gate, and safely left our 1999 Christmas tree in the backyard.

"Miss Walter, I'm here to escort you inside to listen to fine country music and conversation," I said after opening her car door. We strolled to the house with our arms clasped around each other's shoulders, and I sang, "I bought one bottle of ketchup on a two-for-one night. No need to waste money on another tomato delight."

We walked up the steps, and I stopped, looked to the moon in the clearing sky, and continued, "Betsy Walter, tonight, under the moon-light, you're the most beautiful sight."

Betsy's face beamed.

We entered the house and planted ourselves on the white couch in the living room. I powered up the stereo and turned to our favorite country music station. We talked about Hannah. A favorite tune wafted its way through the dining room, around the wall, up the split level, past my man chair, and over the white couch, adding to the already romantic ambiance and warming our totally toasty hearts.

My custom dimmer lights helped project even more of a romantic vibe with the perfect not-too-low-or-high setting.

"I've never kissed an alien from Pluto," Betsy said.

"I've never kissed a human who drove a Saturn."

We lay horizontally, almost in sync, kissed for several minutes, and then talked more about Hannah. I daydreamed about taking Betsy upstairs to try to conceive Hannah.

"I love you, Bets," I said. Her eyes rolled upward in bliss, her small, precious head swayed in stupor, and she snuggled onto my chest. Neurotransmitters by the millions delivered electrical signals, providing chills and feelings of joy throughout all pathways and into my soul.

She looked at me. "I love you, too." Then she looked away and turned back with a pained look. "I don't think this is going to work out," she said meekly.

"Why?" I asked, completely caught off guard.

"I just don't think this is going to work out."

I realized where she was coming from. She was a twenty-one-year-old college freshman, and I was a forty-two-year-old father of three. She was in love but overwhelmed and frightened.

I went into save-the-relationship mode. "Honey, I understand." I paused, spoke slowly without projecting pressure, and confidently said, "No relationship is easy. Easy is boring." I took her hands and said, "We've got something special that gets better each time we're together. I'm confident the right thing to do is to keep moving forward. As a couple, we rock."

"Chris, I understand. I've never been happier. This is absolutely what I desire and what I'm going to let myself have."

I looked at Betsy and smiled. "Just breathe." We both took long, deep breaths.

She held me tightly, her body language saying everything would be fine.

Any relationship insecurities we had vanished and never returned. We sank into another intimate moment that lasted an hour —lying there, talking about Hannah, kissing, and cuddling.

4

Y2K FEARS AND A WEDDING PROPOSAL

December 31, 1999

After months of anticipating the potential chaos a widespread computer programming shortcut—known as the Y2K bug—could cause as the year changed from 1999 to 2000, the much-hyped Y2K event was a mere twelve hours away. This significant transition marked the turn of the millennium and was feared to disrupt computer systems worldwide.

The world was ready to "Party Like It's 1999" while the media portrayed catastrophe, suggesting computers would be so confused they could shut down completely. Some reported that the Y2K computer bug would bring an end to modern society.

Despite the sensationalistic media reports, we remained unfazed and decided to spend New Year's Eve on the Pacific Coast. Betsy arrived at noon on a cloudy, chilly day. It might have been a lovely, autumn-like afternoon for New Yorkers, but fifty-five sunless degrees was winter weather for us Northern Californians.

We took State 17 south to Santa Cruz and passed under the bridge at Summit Road (elevation 1,781 feet)—a peak of the Santa Cruz Mountains—singing the Beach Boys's "Surfing USA." Our moods were carefree; we had no worries or hurries. Random passersby waved and gave thumbs-up to the crooning couple.

After crossing the summit, a steep, long, horseshoe curve—Big Moody Curve—veered to the right, revealing breathtaking vistas of the mighty Pacific Ocean, surrounded by dreary skies and heavy clouds gathered in massed ranks. The Monterey Peninsula, a coastal gem that includes the resort community of Pebble Beach forty miles in the background, jutted toward Japan, a sight that could only be described as awe-inspiring.

Vincent van Gogh might have captured the gorgeous gloom in a painting—a dark sky, a cold ocean surrounded by mountain ridges and rainy redwood forests, and cars with burnt-out faces lined in pain, driving over the hill for respite from their lousy lives.

State 17 winds out of the mountains and ends at California State Route 1 in Santa Cruz. We took Highway 1 north to Cruz Coffee, a small, cozy café a friend had suggested. We parked on the side of the building that featured a rich, colorful mural painted with dark purple. Its stormy seas and tie-dyed cups of coffee and tea, unbattered in heavy winds, enveloped the entire outside back wall. The title read, "Coffee Withstands All Storms."

As we stepped into the café, a lively atmosphere greeted us. The sound of steaming milk and the rich aroma of freshly brewed coffee filled the air. We found a cozy spot, sat down, and sipped hot chai, our signature go-to coffeehouse drink. Unlike many places that served a too-sweet version, this café crafted the real deal—a chai latte brewed with two bags of pure, quality chai, easy on the milk, and without added sugar.

Our hands melded together as we sat, as if on autopilot, and the playful battle began.

"We'll soon be headed to Natural Bridges State Beach, about two miles north," I told Betsy. "We'll hike two miles along Cliff Drive on the wide walking-and-bike path that overlooks the ocean below to Lighthouse Point and back."

After several minutes of flirting in a language more potent than spoken words, our thumbs detached. We stood up, and I left two dollars on the table before heading to our car.

Once we arrived at our destination, we parked and walked to the cliff overlooking Natural Bridges State Beach. Several folks had gathered facing the ocean, and a ranger explained what was going on. "This is prime time to see migrating whales." He pointed as two enormous humpback whales jumped out of the water. Like synchronized swimmers, their sleek, streamlined bodies elegantly turned toward us, then landed with a mighty backsplash that would have doused a fire in a two-story apartment building.

"That was spectacular," Betsy said.

"Today's adventure continues. Follow me." We headed toward Cliff Drive and our walk through winter.

Time passed quickly as we moved briskly while holding hands and enjoying the nonstop conversation. We passed dozens of walkers and runners in the fresh Pacific air. Pelicans patrolled in perfect unison, and waves crashed into weathered rock ledges below. Two miles later, we arrived at the lighthouse with expansive ocean vistas and surfers below.

"Look at the surfers! It's freezing cold. Why do they do it?" Betsy asked.

"The thrill from catching and riding waves and the salty ocean spray in their faces. Not only is it exhausting and satisfying, but it's also great cardiovascular and strength exercise. They wear wetsuits to retain body heat." I pointed toward the surfers. "Let's head down the stairs and get a better view while strolling along the beach."

We removed our shoes and socks.

"It smells like low tide," Betsy said, noticing the salty, pungent scent.

"I'm so sorry about my foot odor." I purposely sniffed and looked down at my shoes. We laughed, held hands, and passed a sign without reading its message. Later, we discovered what it said: "Beware, sneaker waves can come out of nowhere and catch unwary bystanders by surprise."

Feeling our feet sink into the cool, soft, granular sand blanketing the beach is a privilege most take for granted. The precious puny pieces of soil, rock, and minerals were formed through thousands of years of being pounded by water and weather. I respect the beach's natural beauty like those who covet diamonds and emeralds. Trekking the oceanfront and feeling the natural cushion below is a spiritual experience that, if done regularly, provides resistance that strengthens the arches, ankles, and leg muscles.

We stopped at the shoreline. With our backs to the water, I reached down and dug up a handful of wet sand. Three small sand crabs rushed out from my hands. Betsy jumped, startled.

I said, "They burrow into the sand and spend most of their time there." Then I stood.

Betsy squatted and directed her conversation to the crabs. "You little guys must be unfamiliar with claustrophobia."

I looked to the water and back to the sand to see several crabs running for their lives. The calming ocean noise suddenly changed— as if an unfamiliar energy was approaching. I pivoted as a huge wave that formed out of nowhere crashed toward us.

We turned and dashed through sand crabs, but a water swell plowed into the back of our knees. I face-planted into rushing water and somersaulted uncontrollably through fifty-two-degree seas surging toward the shore. Betsy tumbled in front of me toward the stairs.

Both of us stood, looking and feeling as if we'd exited a washing machine during the spin cycle. Betsy remained unscathed. I did, too, except for a temporary dizzy spell.

"My New Balances are gone!" Betsy cried out.

Our footwear was no longer on the beach.

"They're being dragged out to sea," Betsy said, pointing to our shoes.

I impulsively removed my sweatshirt and dove into the cold ocean water.

Betsy's shoes seemed to slow down as I grabbed for them, but my body started moving much faster than her shoes. Suddenly, I was ten yards past them and heading toward Hawaii. *It's a riptide!* Instead of saving our shoes, I needed to save myself.

I'd read about getting out of the grip of a rip current. Without panicking, I long-stroked to the left—and it seemed never-ending. I didn't want to be shark bait, so I remained calm, turned, and swam in the opposite direction. My energy quickly depleted. *God, please show me out of harm's way.*

The heaviness in my arms slowed my efforts. I kicked my legs a few lengths, then tried swimming, but my arms had nothing. My head bobbed underwater. I came up and took a breath before a wave knocked me back underwater, forcing a mouthful of salt water down my throat. My body twisted as the current circulated, flipping me on my back and sending me toward Betsy. A shoe hit my hand, and I grabbed it.

I stood up, holding Betsy's left shoe out of the water. Muddy sand filled every crease in my pants and underpants. I was spent—like I'd just swam a marathon—but relieved to have survived that.

Betsy didn't notice my plight. Everything happened so fast while she talked to another drenched couple. We were both soaking wet but alive and well.

"Our sneakers were victims of a sneaker wave," I said, holding Betsy's half pair of New Balances.

"Let's go home." She shook her head and started walking.

The magnitude of my achievement hit me, and I felt great, invigorated, and alive. "Harrison and Hendrix are home. They're going to love this story."

We trashed the solo shoe, walked shoelessly up the stairs, then two miles back to the car, arm in arm—rehashing, laughing, and trying to keep each other warm. The temperature had dipped into the upper forties.

When we saw the car, we bolted for it. I started it up, and the vents spewed out cold air.

"It's freezing," Betsy yelled.

"Be patient. Hot air is coming to our rescue."

Ninety seconds later, delicious hot air blew onto our feet and faces. Betsy's head rested on my right shoulder for thirty-five minutes until we exited onto Camden Avenue, close to home.

"I'd like to make dinner for the boys and us," Betsy insisted as we exited State 17.

"We'd love that."

"It'll be great practice for when we have Hannah."

"Yes, it's important for Hannah to have well-rehearsed parents, including the world's best mom."

"And the best dad."

We parked, exited the car, and entered Lucky's Market. Betsy snatched the ingredients needed for spinach lasagna, the boys' favorite, with New York-style Italian chicken cutlets as a side.

"Should we include some New Year's Eve desserts?" she asked.

"A six-pack of Diet Pepsi and Rocky Road ice cream for dessert. That should do it."

I placed our items onto the conveyor belt behind the checkout divider.

"Are you still enjoying your one bottle of ketchup, Mr. Hennessy?" the checker asked, then laughed.

I looked at him with surprise. "You were here?"

"I was the cashier two registers down. We've talked more about your ketchup song than Y2K," he said, still chuckling.

"That's hilarious. Thanks so much." I fist-bumped him. "We'll see you next year."

"Happy New Year. We'll see you two soon."

As I walked out the door, I looked forward to getting my cold, salty, sandy self—dried seaweed and moist sand chunks in my under-pants—home and into the shower.

We jogged to the car, I placed the bag of groceries in the back seat, and we headed home. Three minutes later, at around 5 p.m., we pulled into my driveway. Thank God Betsy had a change of clothes in her car. She showered in the downstairs guest bathroom and then happily got to work in the kitchen.

After nearly drowning in the cold Pacific Ocean and walking shoeless and wet for two miles in forty-eight windy degrees, I had well-earned a gushing, hot shower. I headed upstairs to my bedroom and into a hot cleansing session, washing the filth off my body and then toweling myself dry. Now clean, invigorated, and relaxed, I was ready for a fabulous night. I headed downstairs and inhaled the aroma of homemade Italian food. The boys and Betsy were talking in the kitchen.

"Please take your seats in the dining room," Betsy announced. She then informed me that Harrison and Hendrix had already set the table and filled our crystal glasses with water.

As we stood at our chairs, I lifted my large glass of reverse osmosis water and said, "I propose a toast."

"Why don't you lead us in prayer first?" Betsy asked.

I lowered my head. "Father God, thank you for bringing us together with fine food and fellowship. When the clocks turn to midnight, please keep our world safe and without issue. Amen." I lifted my head and glass. "Here's to a fabulous night and new millennium. I love you guys. Happy New Year."

The four of us clanked our glasses together, each offering love and well wishes.

Betsy had prepared the first of hundreds of meals she'd serve to my growing teenage boys and me. We dined like Italian royalty and enjoyed conversation and laughter. Obviously, the boys liked Betsy and enjoyed hanging out with us.

"What time are Ryan and Marcus coming?" I asked. I assumed their close friends were coming over, as they did almost every weekend and school holiday.

"They're due in about an hour," Hendrix said, then turned to Betsy. "But that usually means anywhere between sixty and ninety minutes."

"How long have they been your friends?" Betsy asked.

"Since first grade," Harrison said. "We became close friends in fourth grade when we played on the same basketball team."

Hendrix piped in. "We've been on the same team ever since, and we're currently together on our middle school basketball team."

"What grade are you in?"

"We're at Dartmouth Middle School. I'm in seventh grade," Hendrix answered. "Harrison, Marcus, and Ryan are in eighth grade, but they act like little baby third graders."

Betsy and I laughed hard at his comment.

"Hendrix looks like a third grader," Harrison said, pinching Hendrix's cheek. "You're such a cute little buddy boy."

Buddy Boy had been my nickname for Hendrix since he was a toddler.

I made a dramatic gesture toward my sons. "Welcome to the Harrison and Hendrix comedy hour. Now, you two need to hug and make up." I laughed, obviously joking.

"You guys are typical brothers." Betsy chuckled. "My brothers, Joe and Tim, a senior in high school and a freshman in college, are funny like you guys."

"I can vouch for that," I said. "They heckle each other like professional basketball players while playing Nerf basketball in their parent's living room. The games are hilarious and fun to watch."

Betsy gave them an invitation. "You two will have to come to my parent's place near the university in Davis to meet my brothers and parents. It's less than a two-hour drive."

"We'd enjoy that." Harrison wasted no time accepting. "Thanks so much for a wonderful meal."

Hendrix nodded. "It was excellent, Betsy."

"That was a spectacular dinner with great company. Thanks, Bets," I said. "I'm envisioning a two-on-two Nerf basketball game in Davis. Harrison and Joe versus Tim and Hendrix."

"I'd pay to watch," Betsy said, getting up from the table. "I'll clean the kitchen. You guys go outside and play."

Harrison opened the sliding glass door, and we walked onto the deck that overlooked the basketball hoop and putting green. We each picked up a putter and a couple of golf balls and engaged in our usual putting green contest.

Hedrix sank a ten-foot, downhill putt that broke about three feet to the left before circling around the entire cup, stopping on the lip for one split second, and dropping in for the win.

"That's in the hole! Holy moly, Buddy Boy wins another one," I announced.

We put our clubs down, and Harrison high-fived Hendrix. "Okay, little Buddy Boy, now you're going down."

Harrison picked up a basketball, held it in both hands, cocked his wrists, quickly jumped, released the ball at the peak of his jump, and swished it from our three-point line.

The boys chest-bumped, and Betsy came out clapping just as Ryan and Marcus opened the back gate. I introduced Betsy to my boys' best friends.

"You four are stars on the Dartmouth basketball team," Betsy said. "I'd like to see some of the games."

Harrison smiled. "We'd love you to come watch."

Betsy quickly earned the admiration of my boys. That winter, we went to every basketball game. She became a huge fan and helped support them in basketball and other endeavors.

With Betsy, there was no gossip, jealousy, foul language, drama, behind-the-back or petty behavior. She conducted communication with my ex-wife while studying at San José State and set a fine example of love and dedication for my family.

The boys had countless weekend and summer-night sleepovers. Betsy usually made us dinner. Later, Marcus reclined in my Lazy Boy, Harrison was typically half off the couch, and Hendrix and Ryan slept on the floor in sleeping bags. I enjoyed getting up early and spoiling them with a hot breakfast. Through the years, I crafted hundreds of San Francisco sourdough bread loaves into fine French toast, and offered a side of orange juice and occasionally bacon.

I overheard the boys and their friends talk about how it was cool that I scored a young hottie. My kids and I never discussed the age difference. They knew Betsy was a dedicated, friendly, supportive adult figure—in many ways older and more mature than their dad could ever be. Betsy and I encouraged and uplifted the boys and my daughter, Hadley, to be the best version of themselves. At some point within the next few years, we'd hoped to conceive and raise Hannah with similar values.

I picked up the ball and bounced it to Harrison. "Betsy and I are heading inside."

Harrison caught the ball without looking and turned to the others. "Ryan and me versus Hendrix and Marcus."

"Let's do this," Marcus said.

The four boys engaged in a two-on-two basketball game. Betsy and I watched for several minutes, then went inside to our favorite couch.

"The energy of those kids is amazing. They could play that game all night," Betsy said.

I agreed. "They've won many basketball games together. You're going to enjoy the Dartmouth games. There's always a large, supportive crowd, and Ryan and Marcus's parents are great to hang out with."

Hadley and her boyfriend dropped by after the boys came inside at 10 p.m., and the party began. We went down the split level into the TV room and carried water bottles and Diet Pepsi cans.

Betsy had baked the first of infinity batches of her original dark chocolate chip oatmeal cookies with no added sugar. She placed three cookies each in four bowls, added two scoops of Rocky Road ice cream on top, and served the boys. I slowly munched on several delicious cookies while Betsy enjoyed only two, always practicing portion control.

As the new year approached, the countdown began from ten. At zero, we jumped, shook hands, and hugged. Betsy and I kissed while fireworks erupted in the neighborhood. "That was for you and Hannah," I said.

The clocks turned over on January 1, 2000, and we entered the new millennium. There were no computer disruptions. However, the earth may have missed a final opportunity to maintain a society less dependent on computers and technology.

Summer 2000

I never doubted whether Betsy and I would be together. Soon after we met, I trashed my little black book. Betsy was athletic, health-minded, beautiful on the outside and inside, and helped our family function better than I could have without her. We decided that marriage was what we wanted, and we hoped to eventually have one child, Hannah Hennessy. Her parents gave me their blessing.

I planned a surprise proposal during an upcoming walk on our beloved trail. Betsy and I would start at Lake Almaden and hike to the Los Alamitos Bridge. Hadley, Harrison, and Hendrix, and my best friend, Jordan, would reveal themselves from behind the bushes on the other side of the bridge, where I'd pop the big question.

Harrison would film the festivities as Hendrix and Hadley handed each of us a bottle of fresh spring water, and Jordan would present me with the ring box.

On August 8, 2000, at approximately 4 p.m., Betsy and I parked at Lake Almaden, exited our car, and headed toward the trail. Strolling by the lake on an eighty-degree, windless, sunny afternoon made for the perfect ambiance to ask my soon-to-be fiancée to marry me.

A tremendous prehistoric-looking bird, a California condor, glided majestically through a gap high up in the redwood trees toward the creek and passed right over the trail entrance. My eyes did a double take when I noticed an enormous obstacle in front of us— a twenty-foot-high chain-link fence blocking our way onto the trail. The sign read, "Closed for Construction."

"It looks like the entrance to Jurassic Park," Betsy said.

That wicked curve ball threw me into a befuddled state. "You have got to be kidding me," I said, dumbfounded. I'd walked the trail hundreds of times without issue. "Please tell me that fence is a mirage." I closed my eyes and covered my face in my hands. *What to do now?*

Betsy approached and touched the fence. "It's real metal." She came over, looked at me, and smiled. "Chris, it's not a big deal. Let's turn around and walk the lake today."

"I'm worried there may be an obstacle on that trail, too."

"You mean dinosaurs? Seriously, babe, maybe today's walk wasn't meant to be."

The only thing on my mind was asking Betsy to marry me and presenting the engagement ring. Nobody or any equipment was in sight.

"There, did you hear that?" I asked, placing my right hand on my right ear and looking toward the opposite side of the fence. "Listen. The other side is calling." I turned and seriously looked at Betsy. "That's our sign. We need to give this walk a shot."

Betsy shrugged and nodded.

Scaling fences was a favorite challenge when I was twelve. At forty-three, it wasn't nearly as tempting.

Betsy reached the top of the fence in ten seconds. She guided her right foot over the top rail, maneuvered it into an open link, and then another before rapidly descending foot after foot to the bottom and onto the ground.

"Good Lord, that was intimidating," I said. "You couldn't have pole-vaulted over the fence much faster."

"Chris, this is the other side calling," Betsy sang. "We'd really like to have you on our side."

You're forty-three, not seventy-three. Climb the fence. I put my head down, grabbed metal links, and carefully scaled to the top in about sixty seconds. "That was a much easier climb in 1970," I yelled to Betsy. I negotiated my way carefully over the top and down at a similar pace, then stopped about three-quarters of the way.

"Just a couple more links, and you'll be able to jump."

I followed her directions.

"Point your feet and knees forward, bend your knees, jump, and land on the balls of your feet."

I needed to digest those directions clearly. I jumped and tumbled like a human tumbleweed into a Russian thistle—a plant that dies, dries, and turns into a tumbleweed. "Ouch."

"You didn't land on the balls of your feet," Betsy cried out.

"I didn't know my feet had balls," I said, standing up, wiping dirt, and pulling thistles from my clothes.

I looked at my watch. We were about ten minutes behind schedule. I wanted to make up a little time, so I grabbed Betsy's hand and walked briskly, continuing our journey toward engagement.

"The church up the block from the bridge is where Cornerstone, a Christian preschool, is located. We should eventually investigate their programs for Hannah," Betsy said.

"That's a definite on our Hannah to-do list."

The trail was desolate. We were at the top of a small hill featuring vistas overlooking Almaden Valley, about a half-mile away from the most memorable moments of our lives.

"It's a blessing to walk through our pristine, quiet, happy place together," Betsy said.

My adrenaline raced with nervous energy. "What a fabulous view of the bridge. It's a National Historic Landmark, built in the late 1800s, when they began mining mercury up in the hills."

Out of the corner of my eye, I noticed movement about thirty yards ahead in the bushes along the creek. I assumed it was Harrison or Hendrix, scouting our whereabouts. *No, that's a deer.* They're quite common on the trail. I focused more, and a large, sleek, lithe body was camouflaged between bushes. It was another obstacle—a mountain lion.

I'd heard about these beasts for years but had never seen one. Last week's news report mentioned a mountain lion spotted in nearby Almaden Quicksilver County Park.

I grabbed a large stick and Betsy's jittery hand. "I'm so sorry," I whispered. "It's a mountain lion. Stand tall and still, and don't take your eyes off it. We can't appear afraid." *Maybe the closed trail was a mountain lion warning, and I'd walked Betsy directly into harm's way.*

The lion casually swaggered from the brush to the middle of the trail, turned, and looked toward us. I never imagined I'd be staring down the king of the forest. *What are the chances of a lion standing directly in the way of our engagement?* Betsy and I acted unafraid on the outside; inside, we were terrified. I lost control of my bladder. Betsy's sweaty, freezing-cold hand squeezed mine, and she gasped, putting her left hand over her mouth.

That poised animal was magnificent. She wore her smart-looking, golden fur coat with more pride than anyone in human-made material. Those large, striking hazelnut eyes were merely looking to survive in the wilderness, her home.

Her small head made its intimidating body appear twenty feet long. Her thick, tight legs looked powerful like an NFL fullback. The lion opened its mouth and grimaced, either yawning or preparing to attack.

I cringed with apprehension when I saw those large, ugly, never-been-cleaned molars that she used for stabbing, tearing, and eating the flesh of her prey.

I knew the mountain lion would win if we approached, turned our backs on it, tried to run away, or started a chase. They can sprint up to 50 mph and leap forty feet, about ten feet beyond the human world record.

They only come that far from the hills if they can't find food. I didn't want us to be food. I wanted us to travel to the bridge, not through that lion's digestive system.

Functioning in trepidation under such unusual and unfamiliar circumstances presented an unwanted challenge. I cracked my knuckles and took a deep breath. *I've got to figure this out.*

Mountain lions use the element of surprise, which is precisely what I planned to do. I whispered to Betsy, who appeared close to a breakdown. "Scream loud with me, now. Ahh! Yee haw!" We waved our arms wildly. I puckered my lips, curled my tongue up and under my top teeth, and sent a loud, shrieking whistle that echoed in the distance, bouncing throughout the nearby hills.

The startled lion turned and accelerated lightning fast, then disappeared deep into the woods. I stood static, feeling gross in my soggy, sweaty clothing combined with urine, dirt, and thistles. My underarms reeked like a chimpanzee. Victoriously, I fist-pumped the air and turned to fist-bump Betsy, who was in no condition to celebrate. She looked like a frightened character in a horror movie.

"Are you okay?" I asked, even though I knew she wasn't.

Betsy stood stone-faced, crying. "I want to go back to the car," she said, shivering and obviously petrified. "I'm scared."

We hugged like our lives depended on it. Betsy's entire body trembled. In an attempt to soothe her, I placed my right hand on her back, slowly and firmly rubbed it, and spoke gently. "That little lion is more afraid of us and is back in the hills now. We're out of danger. I love you."

If we weren't about to experience our engagement, I'd turn us around and jog back to the lake. "Let's get going to the bridge," I said.

"I want to go back. I want to go back," she said, continuously turning her head back and forth.

I considered coming clean about what was in store over the bridge. *Screw the surprise. We're still getting engaged.*

"Betsy, look at me." I squeezed her shoulders with both hands and said, "We're less than a half mile from the bridge. When we get there—"

"I'm cool. Take me to the bridge."

We proceeded forward. *Thank God.*

Picking up the pace, we arrived at the bridge seven minutes later. I stopped and looked at Betsy. The coloring had returned to her face.

"I'm fine." She smiled. "I can't wait to tell Hannah about that one."

"Mom and I were almost eaten by a lion" *about ten minutes before we got engaged.* I turned to Betsy and chuckled as I thought about how I'd tell the story.

"Dad came to the rescue with his big mouth." We both laughed in disbelief at what had transpired.

We walked under the massive stone arch and across Los Alamitos Bridge. There were two options—turn right toward the parking area or left, and the trail winds into Almaden. We took a right and planted where we usually stretch before turning around. Out from behind the brush, the gang came parading toward us. Betsy's bewildered, perplexed facial expression was priceless.

Hendrix handed Betsy an unopened bottle of fresh, cold water. Hadley handed one to me, and Jordan presented the small box.

I got down on one knee and held the box toward Betsy. "Betsy, you mean so much to me and my family. I'm a better man with you."

Betsy crumpled to her knees, bawling.

"I'd be honored to always be by each other's side. Will you marry me, Betsy Walter?" I asked, opening the case and revealing the ring.

Her sobby, smiling, filthy, sweaty, mascara-smeared-everywhere face gushed with emotion.

I placed the ring on the fourth finger of her left hand.

Through joyful tears, moments after fearing for her life, she looked into my eyes. "Yes, Chris Hennessy," she said with her face inches from mine, "I will be proud to become Mrs. Betsy Hennessy."

"I now pronounce you two engaged," Jordan blurted out.

Our first kiss as an engaged couple led to an ovation of optimism, with our group emitting laughter, cheers, and love. Jordan and I hugged. Hadley and Hendrix embraced Betsy. Harrison and my favorite professional film camera gracefully moved with the action, getting shots from the best angles.

Cold water splashed onto the back of my head, then down my neck, shirt, and into my pants. Hendrix had poured Betsy's bottle of water over my head. After the initial shock, it felt refreshing.

A small crowd gathered, and cars stopped. Someone claimed we were filming a scene for the popular TV show *Survivor*. If Harrison had been with us all afternoon, we'd have all the footage needed for an epic episode.

I turned toward the onlookers. "That's one large step for this man and one giant ring to my woman," I said, then hugged Betsy. The small army around us erupted in appreciation for my romantic antics.

"You got all that?" I asked, pointing to Harrison.

"Got it, Pops," Harrison said with two thumbs up.

"Cut," I ordered in my professional film voice, scissoring two fingers on my right hand. "That's a wrap."

5

UNFORGETTABLE WEDDING DAY ADVENTURES

January 3, 2003

Our bridesmaids and groomsmen had been scheduled to begin processing down the aisle at 4 p.m. at Calvary, our church in San José, a place that holds special significance for us. Just two hours earlier, unexpected circumstances put starting anywhere close to 4:00 in serious jeopardy.

The guys and I arrived at the church at 3:30. I stepped out of my car, as did my sons, Harrison and Hendrix, who were my best men. They looked dapper in their black tuxedos with silver vests and long silver ties. We also sported new black Nike track shoes with neon blue laces, a unique touch to our formal attire.

Betsy had chosen Leigh, her best friend since first grade, as her maid of honor. My daughter, Hadley, was one of four beautiful bridesmaids.

Betsy's manicure appointment was supposed to conclude at 1:30, but it was 2:45 when she headed out to her car. The hairstylist was next—her last appointment. Betsy's longtime stylist, Brandy, had finished with the bridesmaids and waited for the bride at the hotel.

Here's what happened in Betsy's own words:

I realized my wallet was back in the pedicure chair. I got out of my vehicle, and as the car door slammed shut, I saw my keys in the ignition and screamed. The doors locked, with the car idling. I ran into the salon. The manicurist handed me my wallet. I asked to use their phone and called AAA, who said it would take at least an hour for a tow truck driver to arrive.

I walked outside in a panic, totally frustrated and in disbelief at the unfolding situation, and wondered if I would make it to my wedding.

A police car pulled up with emergency blue-and-red lights flashing right next to my idling vehicle. I looked at the sign to see if I'd parked illegally.

"Good afternoon. Is this your car?" the officer asked as he exited his car.

"Yes, it is. Is there a problem, officer?"

"I need to see your ID," he said sternly.

I fumbled through my purse, found it, and handed my license to the officer.

"Please face your car and place both hands on the vehicle," he said, looking at my license. "You and your car match the description of a robbery that happened twenty minutes ago."

"Officer, I've been in the salon the past hour." I had yet to learn what was going on or why.

"May I ask why your car is running?" the officer asked. He turned and walked to his car to take a call from his police radio. He reached into his driver's side window and grabbed the unit.

Could this be a practical joke? Chris might do something like this to a guy friend on his wedding day, and all the guys would think it was hilarious. He wouldn't prank me on my wedding day. I looked around but didn't notice anybody or anything familiar.

I imagined driving past our church in the police car on the way to the police station and seeing everyone out front. I never popped pills, but right now I deserved a couple of Valium. *Father God, please help resolve this terrible situation so we can be married today.*

The officer finished the call, turned, and walked toward me. I closed my eyes, ready for more bad news.

"I'm sorry, ma'am. The perpetrator has been apprehended along with her vehicle."

A universe of stress and worry lifted instantly.

"Officer, it's my wedding day. I just finished with my nails, and I'm locked out of my car. That's why it's running."

"Have you notified anybody?"

"Yes, AAA, but they won't be here for an hour. The wedding is at 4:00."

"Where are you trying to get to?"

"The Los Gatos Lodge."

"Okay, that's twelve to fifteen minutes. I suggest you get in my car. On the way to the hotel, we'll call AAA and make sure they attend to your vehicle. I'll get us to Los Gatos Lodge in twelve minutes."

Chris's dad is a retired NYPD officer, and he taught me that police officers do much more than fight crime. They also help people in arduous situations. If I didn't accept this officer's help, my wedding would be over an hour late.

"A ride would be great," I told the policeman.

I got into the backseat—my first time in a police car. The cop's soothing nature and his efforts to help took away my stress. I closed my eyes and relaxed as tranquility pacified my soul.

At 3:15, the police car pulled up to the hotel. My parents were outside waiting and had no idea I was in the back seat.

Mom and Dad thought they were about to witness a criminal. When I got out of the car, Mom shrieked, then gasped with her mouth wide open.

"Are you okay?" Mom yelled, visibly upset.

"I'm fine. Everything is good. I'm running late and needed a police escort. Every bride dreams of getting a police escort to her hair appointment, doesn't she?" I looked in my purse and found my room key. "Let's jet upstairs to Brandy. I'll tell you the real story later."

I ran over to the police car. "Thank you so much for the lift. It was a godsend."

"My pleasure. I'm so excited for you. Have a fabulous day." The officer saluted and pulled off.

When I finally sat with Brandy, she said, "Betsy, this is a piece of cake. One bride arrived to me at 6:00 for her 6 o'clock wedding." She laughed. "I promise you'll be in the limo by 3:50." (It was a ten-minute drive to the church.) "I'll have your hair at its absolute best. You're going to be the most gorgeous female in San José tonight, hands down."

Brandy moved her hands with maximum dexterity, like the artist and total professional she was, and engaged in only a little conversation, which was not typical for a Brandy hair-do session.

She was done with me at 3:45. The bridesmaids were already in the limo. My parents and I rushed down the stairs and exited the hotel. Mom gasped again, and Dad removed the pipe from his mouth. "Hey, Mom," he said, "is there something you and Betsy haven't told me?"

The same police officer sat in his car, another officer was in her patrol car, and a police motorcycle surrounded the limo.

"Let's get the bride to the church on time, safely and fashionably," the officer said. The police vehicles led the way, and the motorcycle cop acted as our caboose.

Cars pulled over to the side of the road as if we were parting the Red Sea. The girls and I sang joyously all the way to the church.

Our convoy pulled up to the church at precisely 4 o'clock. I rolled down the reflective window and blew kisses as the officers gave a thumbs-up and drove off to fight crime in Silicon Valley.

The officer's help was a godsend. He was my guardian angel, and his goodwill assured me that all would be fine. I realized the insignificance of my wedding starting late. The guys had arrived. We were all here. That day was about sharing our vows and getting married, witnessed by the special folks in our lives.

Instead of being taken to the bride's room, the church coordinator lined up the wedding party outside the church entrance.

Two fellow videographers had offered to film at no charge. Ted, a local videographer and longtime friend, filmed the limo arrival, while Esther, who had filmed dozens of weddings with and for me, filmed us guys.

A week before the wedding, Ted told me, "You'll stress about the videography all day."

That wasn't going to happen. I was going to relish being at a gig and not working. Those two gracious, highly experienced, professional videographers would get plenty of memorable footage.

Betsy's brother Steve seated her mom, followed by my brother Mike, who seated my parents. Pastor Tim led me out from the back room, in front of the congregation, and up the steps leading to the altar. I remained on the top step, facing the crowd.

The processional began, led by Julia, the twelve-year-old junior bridesmaid, and Parker, the ten-year-old groomsman. Betsy had been their beloved babysitter since they were toddlers.

Couples, one by one, slowly proceeded toward the altar. The guys turned right, came up the steps, and took their places next to me. The girls veered left to the bride's side and formed a line next to Leigh.

"Please stand," Pastor Tim announced, motioning his arms.

The congregation stood and turned toward the back of the church. The organist pressed keys, which drove air through the enormous pipes and spread "Canon in D" throughout the church. The potent beginning of the song gave me chills.

The two grand doors opened, revealing Queen Betsy standing arm in arm with her handsome, proud father.

Her strapless wedding dress artfully showed off her sexy, soft, solid, athletic shoulders and décolletage. A delicate, handmade beading design, from the upper section down the left side, with bridal buttons down the back, melded into a satin train. Betsy's veil didn't wholly hide her radiant face. The antique pearl tiara headband she wore had been worn by Betsy's grandmother at her own wedding.

She was the most gorgeous bride of the thousand weddings I'd filmed. My eyes welled with tears. I looked at my mom and dad and was so happy they could make it from New York.

Confidently and proudly, the bride and her dad strolled to me. "Who presents this bride to be married today?" Pastor Tim asked with a huge smile.

"Her mother and I," Betsy's dad said. He lifted her veil, kissed her on the cheek, and then sat next to her mom.

After a fabulous, short talk, Pastor Tim said, "Would you two turn to face each other and hold hands?" He hesitated, smiled, and asked, "Chris, do you take Betsy as your wife?"

I looked at Tim and then back at Betsy. "Yes," I yelled, many decibels higher than my normal voice. *That was a total choke.* The crowd erupted in laughter, providing comic relief at the perfect time. I'd rather have everyone loose and laughing than uptight and quiet.

"Betsy, do you take Chris as your husband?" Pastor Tim asked.

"Yes, I do," Betsy said flawlessly.

"You must have rehearsed that more than Chris," Tim said, then laughed with the congregation.

After a delightful prayer, Pastor Tim announced, "I now pronounce you Mr. and Mrs. Chris and Betsy Hennessy. Chris, you may kiss your bride."

Betsy and I kissed. I fist-pumped the air, and the crowd went berserk as we turned toward everyone.

"Betsy, let's stand here a couple seconds and take this in," I whispered.

"It's the best moment ever," she said, wiping tears from her eyes and waving to the crowd.

I took her hand, and we slowly recessed down the aisle to the song "Celebrate," interacting with our guests, giving high-fives, fist-bumping, and happily married.

Betsy and her mom had done much work together, and our exquisitely planned wedding ceremony came together with aplomb.

My responsibility was planning the reception. Having attended and filmed several hundred wedding celebrations, I was confident in coordinating our party.

I booked the venue, photographer, videographer, and band. The band's lead singer, Lyndsey, who was also our emcee, and I created the schedule for the evening.

It was rewarding but way more complex than I imagined. Multitasking, including small details like how to get my mom and dad from the church to the reception, was tedious and challenging. I realized how much less stressful it was to focus on the wedding video and no other aspects of the event.

Our reception followed at the historic Los Gatos Opera House. I'd filmed several weddings at this venue and knew our one hundred guests would meld comfortably into its ambiance. The unique architecture and layout—illustrious pressed-metal walls, high ceilings, a classic Victorian design, and a dance floor surrounded by thirteen vineyard tables with satin tablecloths and gold Chiavari ballroom chairs—made for a memorable experience. The upper level overlooked the elegant room below.

At their leisure, our guests enjoyed dinner at four food stations, each with an excellent buffet. The carving station served various fine meats. There were also vegetarian and salad options, pasta and potatoes, and desserts. The bar served soft drinks, filtered water, and excellent California red and white wines enhanced with Riedel drinking vessels.

In October, three months before our special day, Betsy and I were hanging out in a local coffee joint, holding our right hands together in the thumb wrestling position, and conversing about our future, including Hannah.

"A handful of my wedding couples performed a rehearsed first dance," I explained. "It's a classy, upbeat beginning. The crowd always goes bonkers, especially when the couple is introduced and goes right into their first dance. The energy level rarely wanes."

"I love it," Betsy answered enthusiastically.

"Would you take dance lessons with me, Betsy Walter?"

"I certainly will." She excitedly said, "Let's dance to 'Cowboy Take Me Away.'"

"Cowboy Take Me Away" was our romantic anthem song in the early 2000s when Betsy was busy completing her senior year at San José State. (She graduated with a BS in Nutritional Science and Dietetics in June 2003, a few months after we married.)

"Great idea."

"Where will we take lessons?"

"There's a well-known dance studio a few miles from the house. I'll give them a call and set it up," I said. Then I warned her, "I was always quite coordinated with baseball, basketball, golf, or when running. Anything beyond propelling myself forward on foot was way less graceful. I tripped over the soccer ball instead of kicking it, and it looked like I'd twisted both ankles when trying to dance. I've never taken a dance lesson."

"Neither have I." Betsy laughed. "I'm sure you'll be fine between the instructor and me. All great athletes can learn one basic dance. It'll be a blast."

"Thanks, Sugar Plum." Most clever mates come up with one lasting nickname. I've given Betsy many aliases through the years. After we saw *Nutcracker* live, Christmas 2000, Sugar Plum became her first handle. Occasionally, a former nickname, like Bets, sounded better than the one I'd been using. At that time, though, Betsy was my sugar plum.

"Chris, how will the evening progress after our first dance?"

"Your dad will thank our guests for coming to support us and propose a toast. The emcee will invite guests to the food stations. After an hour of enjoying dinner and mingling, The Martin Mangoes Band—the best wedding band in the Bay Area—will have us rocking for about ninety minutes. The band will take a break, and we'll cut the cake. Then you'll throw the bouquet directly into Leigh's single hands."

"Can I do that?"

"You just aim her way and go for it."

She laughed. "Leigh will love that."

"The band will resume. About an hour later, we'll change, return to the room, and do our last dance. We'll leave the guests dancing and drive to Hotel De Anza, where we'll spend the night in the penthouse." (Hotel De Anza is an Art Deco, jazz-age hotel in downtown San José that has been patronized by presidents, first ladies, famous musicians, professional sports teams, and movie stars.)

"Get out of here," Betsy said, delighted. "How on earth did you arrange the penthouse?"

"My longtime friend Alison is the GM. I got to know her in the events industry. This is her and husband Jeff's wedding gift to us."

"Way to go, Alison and Jeff," Betsy said. She clapped, stomped her feet, then high-fived me.

"We've got two nights on top of San José. On Sunday, we'll be with family, and on Monday morning, we'll head to Napa Valley for five nights in the most gorgeous wine country in our solar system."

We arrived at the Almaden Dance Studio the following Tuesday night for our first dance lesson and checked in at the front desk. "Hayden will be your personal dance instructor," the receptionist said. "When you enter the ballroom, you'll see her on the other side of the dance floor."

We entered the ballroom. "Ladies and gentlemen and Hayden," I improvised, "let me introduce you to the soon-to-be Mr. and Mrs. Chris and Betsy Hennessy, two of the worst dancers in Silicon Valley."

Hayden clapped and laughed as she approached us. "That was easily my best client introduction out of hundreds. You two rock."

By her reaction, body language, and voice, I knew that Betsy and I would enjoy dance lessons with her.

I handed her a CD with our song, "Cowboy Take Me Away." It was a five-minute tune, but I edited a two-minute-and-thirty-second version for our dance.

Hayden listened. "I love it. This is going to be a fun adventure," she said and fist-bumped us.

"Let's start. First thing, you two need to get comfortable together. I want you to hold each other and sway back and forth."

I placed my hands around Betsy's lower back, and Betsy's arms were on my shoulders. We stood there together, swaying back and forth several times.

"Great," Hayden said. "Now, let's add some movement."

Hayden taught us a simple box step, and we swayed while dancing around a square.

"Hey, Hay, I just danced. Pinch me." I was pumped. "What's next?"

She choreographed our entrance into the ballroom and onto the dance floor while walking us through it.

"That was creative brilliance," Betsy said.

"When neat, eager-to-learn folks are having fun and willing to put in the effort, my creative juices flow," Hayden said. "Okay, let's do this."

Betsy and I walked into the room, standing tall and holding hands. After stopping at the head of the dance floor, we lifted our clasped hands above our heads. I swung Betsy around me 360 degrees. We glide-stepped to the middle of the dance floor, stood there for two seconds, then pivoted, step-touched left, step-touched right, then front-to-back, and stopped. I improvised a dip and kissed my gorgeous dance partner.

"Yeah, Betsy and Chris!" Hayden screamed and applauded. "I like what I'm seeing."

"Are you talking about Betsy?" I asked. "Because I'm thinking the same thing," I said, softly patting Betsy's butt.

"Dancing is doable when someone is there, teaching and showing us what to do," I said on the way home after our first fabulous, two-hour lesson. "Hayden has already helped me become a bit of a dancer."

"You were excellent. I'm so proud of your focus and determination in accomplishing the intro," Betsy said.

"Thanks, Bets. It was challenging but much fun. It helps to have a good partner. You danced like a pro."

Every class was a fun, challenging, bonding experience for Betsy and me. We gave it our all, two hours per session, and practiced diligently at home. Besides my occasional moments of comical insanity, which helped keep our sanity, we accomplished learning a first dance.

"Alright, you two, let's perform the entire dance," Hayden ordered after we practiced several times during our tenth and final lesson.

Two minutes and thirty seconds flew by fast. Our synchronized, focused flow continued from our first steps until the finish line. I dipped and kissed my sugar plum girl.

"You guys killed that!" Hayden yelled and pumped her fist.

We stood and embraced in a victory hug after showing Hayden what she'd directed us to achieve. "That was the coolest thing I've ever done in sports," I said, gasping for air, as Betsy and I high-fived and held each other.

"That felt like *Dancing with the Stars*," Betsy said, sweat dripping from her forehead.

Hayden came over and joined us. Teary-eyed, she said, "I'm going to miss you guys."

"Hey, Hay," I asked, with the nickname I'd called her. "Betsy and I want to invite you to our wedding to hang out with our gang, eat dinner, drink fine wine, and watch our dance."

"That would be fantastic. I love the Opera House and you two."

"One more thing before we leave," I said. "We would be honored if you'd introduce us at the party."

"You guys are fantastic. I've been to a handful of my couple's weddings," Hayden muttered emotionally. "This will be my first time introducing newlyweds into their party. I'm touched and thrilled."

Hayden was a fun, talented, hilarious dance teacher and became our friend for life.

At the reception, Betsy and I were in the hallway as Lyndsey announced the parents and the wedding party into the ballroom.

"I'm not nervous," Betsy declared, her body trembling with elation.

"Let's savor this moment and the rest of our lives together," I whispered to my wife, our love and connection palpable. Adrenaline surged through my being, a testament to the strength of our bond.

"Next," Lyndsey said, "please get out of your seats, come up, and surround the dance floor."

Our guests, having witnessed our heartfelt ceremony and enjoyed the fine California wine and appetizers, eagerly anticipated our dance performance. They rushed from their seats to the stage, like William Wallace's Scottish resistance forces charging into battle, ready to unleash their excitement.

"I'm going to hand the microphone to Chris and Betsy's dance instructor, Hayden," Lyndsey said.

God's presence and pure goodness immersed me in a fabulous, focused zone. Betsy and I took a deep breath, held it briefly, and exhaled.

Hayden took the mic, smiled at Lyndsey, and turned toward the crowd. "Ladies and gentlemen and fellow wedding attendees," Hayden announced and paused, "I'm proud to kick off tonight's festivities."

Our group erupted, cheering loudly, howling, and screaming out their desire to witness our memorable moment. Betsy and I squeezed hands.

Hayden looked toward the closed doors. "I'm happy to introduce two of my favorite people and the most fun folks I've coached," she paused and pointed at the door, "Mr. and Mrs. Chris Hennessy!"

When the instrumental intro of our song began, the doors swung open, and our loud and rowdy group let loose into pure pandemonium.

We entered, four eyes facing straight ahead, absorbed in the moment, and stopped abruptly at the head of the dance floor. Betsy looked to the left as I peered to the right. We turned to each other. I twirled Betsy around me, and then we stepped straight ahead into our circle of love, cutting through the plethora of positive vibes.

Our synchronized movements and the electric energy of our guests propelled us through one hundred fifty seconds of high intensity. In tune with each other and our dance, we precisely executed every step.

We pivoted, turned face to face, and shared a smile. Then I dipped Betsy down, her head falling toward my knees. Our mouths met in a passionate kiss, a perfect end to our performance.

The place went crazy. Arms waved, hands clapped, and mouths screamed and whistled while precious fermented grape juice spilled down their throats and chins and splashed onto the floor.

"We did it," I said, barely catching my breath. Betsy and I hugged.

"What a rush," Betsy said, perspiring and breathing heavily. "It went by so fast."

"What an incredible beginning to the best night of our lives."

"Amen, baby."

"How cool was that?" Lyndsey declared. "That dance would have made The Dixie Chicks proud. How about giving it up again for Mr. and Mrs. Chris and Betsy Hennessy?"

Our performance earned us a sustained boisterous applause.

"It's only going to get better from here," Lyndsey promised. "Please take your seats." Her hands motioned down. "Betsy's dad will offer a welcome toast in a few minutes."

"You two made me so happy." Hayden surprised us from behind and then hugged us.

"Hey, Hay!" Betsy yelled. "Thanks for the excellent introduction."

"Your confident voice was perfect and uplifting," I said, "and it set the tone for our performance."

"I love you guys." She kissed us each on the cheek and sat at her table.

I pulled out Betsy's chair, and we sat at the head table for the first time.

"This is a magnificent view," she said, looking throughout the room. "The folks, food tables, bar, stage, upstairs. It's fabulous."

"See the cake?" I asked Betsy, pointing at our strawberry-choco-late wedding cake. "If it slides off the table and onto the floor, we don't care. We're surrounded by the most special people in our lives. That's the most important thing."

"Ladies and gents, please make some noise for the bride's father, Denny Walter." Lyndsey gave the mic to Denny and clapped.

"I didn't know Chris could dance," Dad deadpanned with a confused look, getting a great laugh. "Seriously, when Mom and I heard Chris played golf," he paused and looked at me, "we knew he'd fit right in." The crowd guffawed.

"Look at this beautiful bride." He paused again, wiped his tears, and looked at us with a loving expression. "Watching you two warms my heart." He turned toward the crowd, "Chris and Betsy together is a total team effort. Mom and I couldn't be prouder and happier." Dad looked back at us. "Let's raise our glasses to these two fun, brilliant, health-conscious, country-music-loving thumb wrestlers." Glasses clanged, the liquid was gulped, and happiness continued. Betsy and I hugged Dad.

The emcee invited the bridal party and parents to visit the food stations. Betsy and I stacked our plates with gourmet fare, sat, relaxed, and savored our meals.

We planned on walking through the ballroom to greet guests after dinner. Instead, guests consistently came over to greet us, enabling us to stay seated while enjoying the conversation.

"How's the cider, gentlemen?" I asked Harrison and Hendrix. They had walked by several times, holding glasses of what appeared to be sparkling apple cider.

"Hits the spot, Pops," Harrison answered.

"Great dance. We're so happy for you guys," Hendrix said.

"We love you guys so much," Harrison said. He lifted his glass, and both he and Hendrix chugged their beverages.

"Chris, Betsy, wedding party, and all civilians, we need you up to the dance floor," Lyndsey announced. "It's time to get this party started."

Humans entered the dance floor from all directions. The Martin

Mangoes Band went into "Twist and Shout," and we danced the next ninety minutes to top-shelf live music, which, in my opinion, was way more conducive to a great dance party than DJ music.

My friend JD approached and said, "That was the best ceremony, and we're in the middle of the best party, Chris. Congrats to you two. Carol and I wish you much happiness."

We shook hands. "Thank you so much." I noticed his mug of apple cider. "Hey, JD, what are you drinking?"

"Heineken on draft," he said, smiling like he'd just won the lottery, and then he walked back over to his table.

I headed to the bar. "Are we serving beer tonight?" I asked the bartender.

"Yes, Mr. Hennessy. The Opera House threw in complimentary draft beer. It's a small token of our appreciation for the hard work and excellent service you've provided our clients through the years. Your videos are unique and entertaining," the bartender said, expressing his gratitude.

"That's very generous." I shook his hand. "Thank you for your wonderful words."

I turned around and chuckled about my boys, thinking how my brother Jim and I would have done the same at their age. I found them, said, "No more apple ciders," and walked away.

"You two gorgeous people." Betsy's mom put her hands on our shoulders, breaking the moment. "It's past ten. You need to get ready for the last dance."

"Great idea," Betsy said. "Thanks for reminding us, Mom."

We left the reception to change into our dressy casual clothes. Then, holding hands, we walked back into the ballroom, headed toward the dance floor, and received screeches and whistling.

"It's time for Betsy and Chris to dance one last time," Lyndsey announced. "Get the heck up here and surround these two." The crowd cheered and encircled us. "Let's give them the love and send-off they deserve," she said. "Dancing again to their introduction song, 'Cowboy Take Me Away,' here's Chris and Betsy."

Unlike the introduction, in which we danced to the song's recording, Lyndsey performed a live, slower version of "Cowboy Take Me Away" with her husband, Jessi, who played acoustic guitar.

Betsy and I slowly swayed while moving about inside the circle, talking with and fist-bumping folks who offered enough encouragement and well wishes to last a lifetime.

As the song ended, Lyndsey invited the guests to rush to the middle, where we all embraced in a huge group hug.

Everyone was feeling great after a beautiful day. I lifted my wife's left hand and showed off Betsy's ring. The crowd oohed and aahed.

"Okay, babe, it's time." I grabbed Betsy's hand and whisked us from the depths of our circle. We walked briskly out the open doors, through the hallway, and outside into the car, which was ready and running. Thirteen minutes later, we arrived at the Hotel De Anza.

I'd planned Sunday to be a family day. The guys and I were going to play golf at nearby Silver Creek Valley Golf and Country Club. The girls and Mike's kids would hang at the Los Gatos Lodge's pool and Jacuzzi on what was forecast to be a cloudless, seventy-five-degree January day. My New York folks were ecstatic. Spending time outside on Long Island in January was a rare occurrence.

We'd all be together at the Lodge on Sunday evening, swimming, enjoying the Jacuzzi, having a bonfire BBQ, and singing karaoke inside the bar.

On Monday morning, Betsy and I would drop off my family at Oakland Airport, then head to our much-anticipated honeymoon destination, the magnificent Napa Valley, a mere fifty-mile drive. We were both excited about the days of relaxation and exploration ahead.

We checked in at the front desk. The woman explained how to get to our room. "Here's a key to your private elevator. It'll drop you off inside the penthouse."

"If we lose the key, will we be able to get out of the penthouse?" I asked, looking at Betsy.

"We can arrange for you two newlyweds to be locked in." She laughed.

"Great, we'll see you in a couple days," I said as we walked to our elevator.

The elevator doors opened, and we entered the living room. "We're in a movie," Betsy said.

"Wait until you see the bathroom scene." I led Mrs. Hennessy into the grand bathroom.

"It's the size of our house." She was in awe as she sauntered in. "I could live here."

There was a hot tub, a double shower, twin toilets, fine soaps, lotions, shampoos, and enough room for Queen Betsy to be unhurried and uninterrupted.

"It's a shower for two. Let's both go in," I suggested. Feeling the weight of the day, we were utterly exhausted.

Betsy went in. "It feels like a hot waterfall crashing over my head."

"This is heaven," I said, joining her. The warmth and force of the water provided a cleansing massage. We lathered each other with soap and shampoo, then scrubbed, rinsed off, and got out.

The quick-dry cotton bath towels sponged up the remnants of my shower in seconds. Feeling immaculate made it easy for me to lie down and relax.

We both surrendered from the hold of gravity, got horizontal, and looked at each other. "We did it, Mr. Hennessy." Betsy smiled and closed her eyes.

"Everything was flawless, Mrs. Hennessy. The guests had a fabulous time."

Betsy didn't answer or move. She was snoring away on our California King bed's satin sheets. I went unconscious a few moments later.

I awakened at 8 a.m. Betsy had already showered and was taking full advantage of the luxurious amenities in the bathroom.

"Good morning, Christopher," Betsy chirped as I entered the bathroom.

"Hey, babes." I gave her a kiss, brushed my teeth, and got dressed.

"I'm going to hang out on the balcony. It's a gorgeous day. Come out when you're done." When Betsy was ready, we'd head downstairs for breakfast in their five-star restaurant.

The balcony overlooked downtown San José. I stepped into the refreshing, windless, winter morning atmosphere, closed my eyes, and let the sun's rays fill my face with medicinal natural light.

After ten minutes, I walked over to a table, stretched my hamstrings, and sucked in delicious, chilly, clean Pacific air.

At twenty minutes, I figured she'd be out anytime. I was ready to eat. It dawned on me that twenty minutes in the restroom should have been enough. I went inside and didn't find Betsy in the bathroom, bedroom, or living room. *Where the heck is Betsy?*

She didn't have a cell phone, but she did have the spare penthouse key. I pushed the elevator button to the first floor, exited, and walked briskly to the restaurant. I looked inside, asked the restaurant hostess, hustled through the hallways, went out on the patio and to the hotel lobby area, and there was no sign of Betsy.

I race-walked to the elevator and took it back up to the penthouse. I looked in every room, even under the bed. A rush of horror flushed through my head and sucked the zest out of my soul. My newly wedded wife was missing!

I hurried down to the first floor, into the lobby, and explained the situation to the front desk agent.

"I'm sorry, Mr. Hennessy. Excuse me for a moment. Let me find the hotel manager." He walked behind the desks and into another office.

I'm sure he sensed my frustration, confusion, and fear. "Mr. Hennessy, we've alerted hotel security to be on the lookout for Betsy. Our security officer will be out to speak to you shortly," the agent said as the security person approached me.

He reached out to shake hands. "Mr. Hennessy, I'm Ken, security at the hotel. Please come with me. We'll take the elevator up to the penthouse."

We entered the elevator. "She was having a grand time getting ready in the restroom," I explained. "I told her I'd wait on the balcony. She was gone when I returned to the bathroom twenty minutes later."

"Which balcony were you on?"

"Which balcony?"

"Yes, sir, there are two."

I took the lead across the living room and out onto the same balcony where I had earlier waited for Betsy. It was empty.

"Follow me." The officer led me inside, across the living room, and into a breezeway, where a less noticeable door led us onto the other balcony.

Betsy was sitting comfortably on a Beachcroft loveseat in the sun, her eyes closed and her headphones blasting country music. She opened her blue eyes, removed and threw down her headphones, stood, and jumped into my arms. "I'm so sorry. I came out of the bathroom and onto this balcony. I didn't realize there were two. I feel like an idiot."

"Neither of us knew there were two balconies. I'm so glad you're okay."

"I went downstairs twice and then figured it would be best to stay put. I knew you'd be here eventually."

"Mr. and Mrs. Hennessy, the Hotel De Anza's website will include a new caution statement," Ken said. "Beware! There are two balconies in the penthouse." He reached into his pocket. "Here's a coupon for a weekend stay in the penthouse and dinner for two at the restaurant. We're so sorry for the confusion, and we hope this makes you happy. We wish you two the very best."

"Thanks so much, Ken. Your professionalism and generosity are much appreciated." I turned to Betsy. "I'm starved. Will you join me for breakfast, Mrs. Hennessy?"

6

THE FERTILITY JOURNEY: TROUBLE TRYING FOR HANNAH

December 2008

Betsy informed me that three years had passed since she'd stopped taking birth control pills. I had no idea we'd been trying that long for Hannah.

It'd been nine years since Whole Foods introduced Betsy to me. She remained the consistently perfect stepmom—no pettiness, drama, or jealousy, and she cared. Upon graduation from San José State, she passed her RD—Registered Dietician—and became a highly respected clinical dietician at Wellbound Dialysis.

We celebrated our fifth wedding anniversary at Carmel Valley, our longtime weekend getaway spot. Harrison and Hendrix were in college. Haddley had graduated from USC and worked as a sportscaster for Fox Sports News. I'd progressed from forty-two years old to fifty-one. Betsy, twenty-one when we met, was now thirty.

I'm as attracted to Betsy today as I was when I saw her sitting in the juice bar area at Whole Foods in Los Gatos, California, on Saturday, November 13, 1999. She's naturally beautiful, like Half Dome's granite face overlooking Yosemite Valley in the dawning daylight.

Betsy starts every day with a hot shower and ends with a hot lava-like bath—even if it's 105 degrees outside. She never misses a day blowing hot, gale-force winds from her Kmart blow-dryer through moist, clean, strawberry-blonde hair. The makeup session follows, even though, in my opinion, she looks fine without it.

"We've been trying to conceive Hannah for three years," Betsy said nonchalantly near the end of her morning rigmarole, catching me by surprise.

We'd enjoyed a plethora of lovemaking sessions for several years. I'd be good with trying a couple more years—it was that enjoyable.

Feeling hopeful and wanting to make our journey to conception a bit more fun, in early 2007 I came up with a game called dollar-in-da-jar. The jar on the nightstand beside our bed received a one-dollar donation after each intercourse session. After a year, that cash would be spent on a getaway weekend in Carmel Valley—a lighthearted way to keep our spirits up and focus on our shared goal.

We had a record year of love in 2007—two hundred twenty-seven dollars' worth. Remarkably, our bed endured all those earthquake-like roller coaster rides. We were hopeful, believing firmly that our love and efforts would bear fruit.

Unfortunately, we didn't get pregnant. Betsy insisted on making doctor appointments to see if any issues held us back. The visits were set for early January 2009.

Because of a harsh illness that resulted in missing much of the eleventh grade, the doctors had warned Betsy she might have issues trying to get pregnant. However, she checked out fine.

Feeling a mix of nerves and anticipation, I walked into my urologist, Doctor Jack's office. The receptionist at the front desk asked, "Do you have an appointment?"

"Yes, I do," I answered. "I can't wait to sit in the chair while the dentist works on my teeth."

She looked at me and didn't say anything for two seconds. "If you thought your dentist was fun, wait until Doctor Jack examines you," she deadpanned.

"You mean this isn't my dentist appointment?" I feigned disappointment as we both shared a hearty laugh. Moments like these, filled with humor, helped me maintain my spirits.

"Mr. Hennessy, please complete this paperwork and provide me your ID and insurance card."

"Impressive," I said. "How did you know my name?"

"I'm good at figuring things out. It's 10 a.m., and there's only one 10 a.m. appointment."

"Brilliant. This office is fortunate to have you."

"Your last name is spelled the same as Hennessy Cognac. Is there a relation?"

"Yes, same spelling, no relation. If there were, I'd be the master taster."

"Mr. Hennessy," she said and giggled, "please sit and fill out the forms."

I sat in the seating area, put the pen to the paper, and chatted with several other patients.

"Mr. Hennessy," the nurse called when she entered the seating area.

I followed her to the doctor's office. A moment later, the doctor arrived. "Hello, Mr. Hennessy. I'm Doctor Jack Wherry. Patients and staff call me Doctor Jack." He reached out his hand and gave a short, firm handshake.

"Doctor Jack, it's a pleasure."

Doctor Jack was a delightful gentleman. I explained our situation. "My wife and I have enjoyed plenty of healthy sex for three years without conceiving."

He didn't seem concerned, and neither was I. "Janey will schedule your follow-up appointment," he said, then looked down at his computer and entered an order for a complete blood count. Please get your blood drawn across the street, and then I'll see you soon."

"Mr. Hennessy," Janey said, handing me the January 30, 2009, appointment card. Her reassuring smile and professional demeanor made me feel cared for. "See you next time."

"You love saying Hennessy, don't you?"

"Yes, I do." She firmly gripped my right hand with hers and gave me a long, confident handshake. "My name is Janey."

"You make coming here more enjoyable, Janey," I said, chuckling. "I'm Chris." Our hands separated.

"Thanks again, Mr. Hennessy," she said, smiling, looking at me.

"It's been a pleasure. I'll see you the next time I see you." I pointed at the door and asked, "Is it okay if I leave?"

"Yes, as long as you return for your next appointment."

I had my blood drawn, then visited Doctor Jack for my follow-up on January 30.

"Good morning, Janey. This is my wife, Queen Betsy," I said, proudly looking at Betsy. "Queen Betsy, this is Janey." I turned and glanced at Janey. "Betsy and Janey," I peered at Janey, then Betsy, "this is each other."

Janey laughed. "It's a pleasure to meet you, Mrs. Hennessy. I can't imagine how and where you found Mr. Hennessy, but we're glad you did." Janey smiled and turned to me. "Doctor Jack will be with you shortly." She turned to Betsy. "Mrs. Hennessy, it's great you're here today." She gave us the peace sign, and we took a seat.

"Chris Hennessy," the nurse called out a minute later.

Betsy followed me toward the nurse, and we stayed behind her to the patient rooms. "Please enter number three," she said, pointing toward room three.

"Oh," I said meekly. "Number three?" I acted out by shrugging, shaking my head, clicking my tongue, and sucking a deep breath in and out. "I'm sorry and embarrassed to mention it." I looked at Betsy as if concerned, then back to the nurse. "But the number three is bad luck for me." I rubbed my forehead. "I was hoping for room one or two. I guess number three is fine." I nodded. "It's simply one plus two. We're all good."

"I don't have my calculator," she said, appearing slightly confused, then she turned and strode into room number three.

Betsy spun around with a nasty face. "Cut it out. This is serious stuff, Chris."

"I'm as serious as Doctor Jack is going to be," I said, still chuckling, and then smiled. "But I'm also going to enjoy myself."

Ad-lib humor was my mental warmup. I thrived when performing improv comedy schtick in real life, on stage, or on camera. Contemplating what to say as I performed a bit—getting laughs and reactions —was self-therapy. It enabled me to focus, understand the doctor, and know how to proceed—all vital to my health and well-being.

I sat, and the nurse wrapped the blood pressure cuff around my left arm.

"Okay, Mr. Hennessy," she said, expressionless. "If you don't calm down, your and my blood pressure readings will be too high." She pressed the button, the cuff gently squeezed my arm, and after several seconds, the LED screen read 128/79. "Perfect, Mr. Hennessy."

"Thank you. I don't rattle easily." I paused. "But good try." Then we both laughed. I sensed the nurse appreciated my antics.

Doctor Jack entered. "Hello, Mr. Hennessy," he said before sitting down, looking at me, and getting to business. "To start, you have a fungus in your sperm. This microorganism affects male fertility potential and could alter oocyte fertilization."

That can't be good.

"Your sperm count is quite low, and your PSA blood test revealed an abnormally high reading of 8.9. The normal range is one through four. This indicates possible prostate cancer."

"I knew my healthy lifestyle would pay off," I said, slightly kidding but primarily upset. Receiving such news was unexpected. I ate healthily, hardly drank alcohol, had never smoked, hydrated properly, and exercised regularly since my teens.

Betsy grabbed my hand and held it tightly.

"Mr. Hennessy, these issues are likely hindering your efforts to conceive."

"What does this mean?" Betsy asked.

"I'll tell you what it means," I interrupted, realizing our plight. "It doesn't look good for having Hannah. We've had unprotected sex hundreds of times without conceiving." I looked straight ahead, dejected, annoyed, and not wanting to believe what we were hearing.

"Mr. Hennessy, let's not jump to any conclusions," Doctor Jack said with conviction. "Having a baby at this point is not impossible. It only takes one strong, healthy swimmer to fertilize Betsy's egg. We'll conduct the PSA blood test and sperm count twice in the next two months and see what the numbers do. I'll see you in two months."

Janey was away from the front when we left, which was fine. I certainly didn't feel up to smiling, talking, or joking around.

We drove home without verbal communication, both stuck in our heads. When ready to talk, I prayed. "Father God, I've worked hard to be healthy and not have to deal with such medical issues. Please bless us with a negative cancer diagnosis and positive news regarding Hannah."

We parked in the driveway, walked with our heads down, and entered the house. Betsy looked shattered and began to cry gently. I hugged her, and she put her head on my shoulder. We were heartsick. Our longtime dream of having Hannah was in serious jeopardy.

April 2, 2009

Since my last meeting with Doctor Jack, I had blood drawn twice. Betsy and I arrived at my follow-up appointment ready for good news.

"Hey, Janey," I said, walking to the front desk.

"Hello, Mr. and Mrs. Hennessy." Janey greeted us with a smile.

"Would it be okay to call him Uncle Doctor Jack?"

"Why?" she asked, chuckling.

I shrugged. "I don't want to call him Aunt Doctor Jack," I answered straight-faced and raised my hands. Janey, the nurse, and a couple of patients laughed enthusiastically.

"As long as your insurance is current," Janey answered, "he won't mind what you call him."

Everyone laughed.

"Room number three again?" I asked the nurse.

"No, Mr. Hennessy. Two minus one."

"Room one. Perfect."

We walked into room one, and the nurse said, "Please have a seat, and I'll take your blood pressure."

"Calling it blood pressure makes me feel pressure. Why not call it blood-without-pressure?"

"That's a great idea," she said, looking at Betsy and rolling her eyes. "I'll have Doctor Jack bring it up at the next American Medical Association National Conference."

"No pressure," I said again and chuckled, and so did she.

"Okay, let me strap on the blood-without-pressure machine." After placing the cuff on my upper arm, she pressed the button, and the cuff began inflating and squeezing my arm tightly, then deflating quickly. "Your blood pressure is 129/81. That's an excellent reading."

"Now, we need Uncle Doctor Jack to give us some good news," I said, pointing at the door.

Waiting for the doctor can be daunting, akin to sitting on the Kingda Ka roller coaster while the attendant ensures everyone's buckled in. When I get terrified, chatting and interacting with humor gets the natural drugs flowing, keeps me out of fight-or-flight, and helps me cope and pay attention. Even though we faced an ocean of stormy seas moving forward, I somehow became confident and fearless.

A few minutes later, Doctor Jack entered and told us that my PSA level had nearly doubled to 18.7 and prostate cancer was likely. He also said my sperm levels weren't conducive to procreating.

He shook his head. "The chances of conceiving a child are unfavorable. I'm so sorry."

"How not favorable?" I asked.

"Very not."

"Very not favorable," I said, enraged. I wanted to fight that diagnosis. Instead, I knew I had to suck it up and move on.

"The next step is to schedule a prostate biopsy in two weeks. Unfortunately, after the biopsy, conceiving will not be possible."

Betsy grimaced, and tears slid down the nurse's cheeks. *My wife may not be able to have Hannah and faces the prospect of losing her husband to cancer.*

"Wait, Doctor Jack," I fired back. "We want to try another month or two for Hannah," I said, looking at Betsy.

Betsy nodded.

Despite the odds, I believed we could become pregnant with Hannah and defeat cancer.

I looked at the nurse. She stared at Betsy, teary-eyed. Betsy's eyes focused on Doctor Jack, who was watching me.

After several seconds, Doctor Jack said, "Waiting a few extra weeks at this point is okay." He smiled gently. "You two go procreate. I'll see you on June 2 for your biopsy."

Betsy and Doctor Jack started discussing the possibility of freezing my sperm. I didn't listen to their conversation. My mind was back on the trail, walking and talking on our first date. *We gazed into each other's eyes, clowned around, and chatted about family, friends, and conceiving a baby we'd name Hannah Hennessy.*

Their conversation ended. I stood tall and shook Doctor Jack's hand. "Thank you, Doctor Jack." I opened the door for Betsy, and we walked to the front desk.

I forced a smile and waved as we passed Janey.

"Take care, you two." She smiled and gave us a thumbs-up.

"I'm scared," Betsy said as we held hands and walked toward the car.

"It's okay to be afraid," I said as we got in the car. "I'm frightened too. Let's turn on music and head to the trail for a walk-and-talk session." Our best conversations took place when we were hiking. "It'll help us digest this and be on the same page moving forward."

Betsy nodded.

We parked, exited the car, clasped hands, and began a therapeutic walk past the lake on a sunny, pleasant afternoon.

"This is where we scaled that gigantic fence on the day we got engaged," I said as we passed through the trail entrance. "Remember how we met up with that wild, hungry mountain lion? We won that standoff battle, and we're going to win these skirmishes too."

"I totally agree," Betsy said.

"Nothing has been diagnosed or prescribed except intercourse. Together, we're going to make Hannah. We must continue to live our lives, cherishing the moments. I love you, baby."

"I love you so much."

We walked over the bridge, stopped, and stretched ten feet from where I'd proposed. I put my head down and grabbed Betsy's hand. "God, please help us to create Hannah. We've talked about her since our first date on this trail nine years ago. Betsy deserves a child as much as anyone, and Hannah will know you as we do."

We hugged, headed back over the bridge, and talked nonstop until we got to my car.

7

NATURE MAGIC ON THE
ARBORETUM TRAIL

Three years off birth control, several hundred sexual encounters, and now we have two months left to try for Hannah, with a low sperm count and likely prostate cancer. The odds were against us, and the upcoming prostate biopsy would bring about permanent infertility.

Months of doctor appointments, medical tests, bad results, waiting on the edge for new developments, and being rewarded with bleak news took a toll on Betsy and me. For the first time, my cave-man-like desire for sex waned considerably. It was akin to arriving home from a loved one's funeral. Sexual arousal, then basking in its physical and psychological loop of pleasure, was not likely to happen.

Betsy used an ovulation predictor kit and basal thermometer to help us conceive. There's a small window each month during which a woman can get pregnant, and these methods help identify the fertile window. The time to engage in intercourse was when the test indicated she was ovulating.

Our back-and-forth banter was like a classic comedic *Saturday Night Live* skit. "Chris, we must do it now!" She pointed toward the bedroom door, panicked.

"Honey, you're way too uptight for lovemaking," I told her.

"Come on, Chris. We're following a program. Are you too uptight to try for Hannah?"

"I'm never too uptight for my Betsy."

"Then get in there and get naked."

We looked at each other, hesitated, and then chuckled.

"This type of behavior takes the natural enjoyment out of it. I have trouble performing after panicked foreplay."

Betsy stood there staring into my eyes for a few seconds, and I calmly waited for a response. She nodded. "You're right. I'm so sorry," she said, whimpering. "I'm afraid. I want us to have Hannah."

I took her in my arms, reached down, held her satin-soft cheeks, and looked at her pained face. "Bets, there's nothing to be sorry about. It was smart to give the new technology a try. I'm sure it has worked for many. Let's throw away those unnatural, expensive kits and make Hannah naturally. The kits make you anxious and neurotic, and that's not going to help us conceive."

Betsy nodded, walked into the bathroom, grabbed the two units, exited the house through the side door, and discarded them into the trash bin.

Moving forward, we engaged in much less sex than usual. When we did, it was pure romance, real love—caring, sensual, and euphoric.

———

"Getaway," I sang out loud to Betsy. "Baby, we need a break from Silicon Valley and our daily routine. Next weekend, we're headed to Mom and Dad's. Not being on a schedule and spending quality time with your quality folks is always a fabulous escape. I've already spoken to Dad and confirmed. They're psyched."

"That's the best idea, perfect timing, and something neat to look forward to. I'm excited. Thanks so much."

Betsy and I had spent many weekend vacations at their large, comfortable house in South Davis, a fine neighborhood where Betsy was raised. It's only an hour-and-a-half drive from San José.

Hiking green belts, strolling the small, charming downtown, visiting our favorite independent coffee house, and then hanging at the bagel joint two doors down were typical favorite activities.

We took off early from work the following Friday and left the house at 1 p.m., easily beating weekend traffic.

Late Saturday morning, after a relaxing conversation-filled breakfast, Betsy's parents, Betsy, and I headed to the meticulously maintained UC Davis Arboretum Trail. This three-mile loop winds along Putah Creek and the campus. Fragrant lavender, rosemary, and other herbs are on both sides of the path. The area teemed with unique plants, trees, birds, ducks, and other waterfowl.

During the delightfully slow first mile, we discussed dinner plans. Dad was going to barbecue turkey burgers and vegetables he'd purchased at the co-op, an independent grocery store for fresh local produce and meats.

Mom and Dad sat on their usual bench with the drooping weeping willow tree barely impeding their pond views. Mom fed the ducks while the scent of Dad's sweet pipe tobacco engulfed Betsy and me as we stretched.

"We're going to head back to our car and then to the store to shop for dinner," Mom explained. "You two continue ahead. We'll meet you back at the house."

"Chris, there's an A's game on this evening," Dad, a longtime Oakland Athletics fan, said, rubbing the palms of his hands like an excited twelve-year-old boy.

I gave him two thumbs up, hugged Mom, took Betsy's hand, and resumed walking through our utopia.

"Father God, the Walter family is such a blessing. Thank you for bringing them and Betsy into my life," I prayed after we'd traversed another mile. "Please give us the perfect time, place, and opportunity to conceive Hannah. I've got the world's best mom-in-waiting. Thank you, Father."

"Father God," Betsy prayed, "Chris is already the best dad, and I know he'll make you and me proud when fathering Hannah. Your help is needed and so very appreciated."

We hugged heartily and continued trekking until we came to a grove of walnut trees in bloom, with plentiful groups of tiny green flowers dangling from sturdy branches. "There are dozens of walnut-less walnut trees," I said. "Where's the walnuts?"

"See all of these," Betsy answered, gently touching the tiny flowers. "They'll eventually turn into walnuts galore."

"Very cool." I nodded. "Betsy, nature is calling. Please excuse me for a couple of moments." I turned and headed toward the opposite side of the trail while she sat on a nearby bench. I found an opening in the heavy brush and walked down a small ravine, which led me through a vine-covered, narrow, cave-like path for about twenty yards. I stepped out of the naturally dark tunnel, and resting below a cloudless, crystal blue sky was a picturesque meadow sprinkled with fields of gold and bright yellow mustard plants.

I looked left and noticed a towering coastal redwood tree protruding three hundred feet high, far above the tree-lined skyline. The trunk seemed as wide as our house and was surrounded by California native blue potato bushes, filled with bright blue-purple flowers and small, daisy-colored dots in the middle. Since moving to Northern California, I have been delighted when walking by homes showing off their vibrant, happy flowers, which remain happily in bloom all year round.

I urinated in the weeds and admired my surroundings. "This is your heaven," I thought I heard a voice say in a flash. Everything felt proper and peaceful. There was no pressure, and nothing else existed except these moments in my outside Shangri-La.

Share this Eden with Betsy. I suddenly felt the need to get back to my wife. I made my way through the cave-like path and up the ravine and broke through the brush, and there was my Queen Betsy. "Woman, you need to see this." I picked her up off the bench. "You're coming with me," I said, carrying my smiling, strawberry-blond Californian girl to the meadow and placing her on her feet.

"This is breathtaking," she said, looking around in awe. It was like the *Wizard of Oz* scene where Dorothy walked out of her house after a tornado ride over the rainbow, and everything changed from black and white to color.

"I am Tarzan," I sang with improvised words and a tune. "I want to swing with you in my arms, Jane. Let's croon duets through the trees, just you and me." I paused. "Please excuse me, I must sneeze." I sneezed, and we laughed at my healthy hilarity.

After an occasional vivid, super-happy childhood dream, I'd awake feeling exhilarating joy and emotional clarity. *This is your heaven.* I assumed the voice was the waking-up part of the dream. I hadn't thought of it in years, but at that moment, I felt it.

Our hands clasped together as we slowly danced to the base of the redwood tree. We gently and comfortably collapsed among beds of vibrant, colorful potato bush flowers, with the sounds of redwood tree branches creaking in the late morning breezes.

My male hormones kicked in—my sexual instinct aroused. What followed was sexual attraction in real-life action. We consummated the best five minutes that neither of us will forget.

"I'd never imagined feeling love as I do now," Betsy said, wiping off her clothes while looking at me. "No pregnancy kits. Good call, Chris."

"Yeehaw, I'm in love!" I swung my fists and sang out, deep amid a glorious, altered state of consciousness. The release of neuromuscular tensions cleansed me like a six-mile run.

We returned to the trail, walked briskly, and talked nonstop for two more miles. Our energetic state of ecstasy continued back to Mom and Dad's house.

Dad had the television turned to the A's game. I sank into their cozy, comfortable couch. Dad and I watched the game as he frequently slipped away to attend to his gas grill outside the sliding glass doors, and Betsy helped Mom in the kitchen.

Mom announced dinner, and we all came in and stood at the table, holding hands, as I offered the mealtime prayer. "Father God, thanks for a safe trip to Davis, our loving family and fellowship, and the fresh food you've provided. Go A's."

We sat, and I passed Betsy the plate of mashed potatoes. "Everything is fresh, delicious, and amazing," I said, looking at her. I turned toward my in-laws. "Thanks so much for having us, Mom and Pops."

"It's our pleasure," Mom answered. "How was the rest of your walk?"

"You two missed out." *Ouch!* Betsy pinched my leg from under the table. She was adamant that no one hear anything about our off-trail excursion. I'd never say anything, but I enjoyed gently teasing her.

8

CELEBRATION AT THE LANDFILL

On Sunday, May 17, 2009, at 3:12 a.m., sixteen days pre-biopsy, I awoke and noticed Betsy sitting in bed, wholly absorbed while carefully studying a tool in her hands. Doing anything but lying sound asleep at this time was highly unusual for her. She was a deep sleeper, rarely up during the night.

I lay still for a few minutes, not caring to move but wondering what was happening. I finally opened my eyes and sat up. "What are you doing?"

Betsy reached over and showed me a device that looked like a thermometer. "Is this a positive result?" she asked with a serious face.

"Didn't we throw those things away?" I mumbled, far from being fully awake.

"Chris, it's a maternity test."

"Really?" I asked, suddenly fully awake and interested. I had never seen a pregnancy test. There were two vertical lines, one bolder red than the other. "I have no idea how this works or what that means."

I read the instructions, which stated, "Two vertical lines, one bolder, are a positive test result." I looked again at the device in Betsy's hands. "It looks positive to me."

Betsy was absorbed in the two vertical lines, perhaps unable to grasp the positive result. "How can we be sure?"

We were caught off guard and not nearly 100 percent convinced.

I suggested, "Let's drive to the 24-hour pharmacy and purchase a different pregnancy kit to confirm."

"That sounds like a smart plan."

We dressed quickly. My T-shirt was inside out, and I wore only socks on my feet. I couldn't find my slippers but didn't care. We drove for two minutes, entered the pharmacy's parking area, and parked. Ours was the only car in sight.

"Let's take this one. It's the cheapest," I said as we looked at many maternity tests in the aisle.

Betsy was reading another box when she turned quickly to look at me. "We're buying this one. I don't care what it costs. And these two," she said and handed me three boxes.

"That's great," I said. "Let's pay and get home."

We bought the three more expensive kits and headed home. Betsy excused herself to the restroom. She came out a couple of minutes later with the three tests. The results would populate in five to ten minutes.

"This is nerve-wracking," Betsy said, holding my hand firmly. No other words were spoken. We held hands and toughed out the wait. Nine years of talking, hoping, praying, and waiting for Hannah had come down to this moment.

After eight minutes, we couldn't resist and checked test number one, which revealed two lines, one bolder than the other, as did numbers two and three. Suddenly, we had no doubts.

"We're pregnant!" Betsy screamed as if she had just won the ten-million-dollar lottery prize.

"Betsy, baby, we did it!" I yelled. "Millions of moments in life aren't remembered, but these moments won't be forgotten. This is so much sweeter than winning the lottery."

That ended our sleep for the night. We cranked up the music and celebrated, dancing and jumping like Hannah would at future bounce-house parties. Excitement filled the house and spilled outside into the completely silent, crisp, wonderfully chilly, 4:25 a.m. air. I cooked pancakes, and we enjoyed a very early and excellent breakfast.

A doctor's appointment soon confirmed the good news—Betsy and Chris Hennessy were pregnant with a baby girl, Hannah Hennessy, due December 7, 2009.

"Every pregnancy is a miracle many take for granted," I told Betsy. "Our Hannah pregnancy is a miracle above and beyond typical gestational miracles. Thank you, God."

Betsy and I began preparing for Hannah the following morning. Betsy worked in Hannah's room, and I uncluttered the garage, digging out of the mess I'd created by putting random boxes everywhere.

Back and forth, I carried our unwanted stuff from the garage to the driveway, dusted it off, and arranged the remaining boxes neatly on the shelves before sweeping the floor. I stood and admired my work. *Ah.*

"You should come and see Hannah's room," Betsy said as she entered the garage. Her eyes and mouth opened wide. "Where has this place been?"

"We should take this load to the garbage dump," I suggested, pointing at the mountain of trash in our driveway.

"Good plan. There's also trash from Hannah's room."

Betsy called her brother Joe, and he dropped off his pickup truck. She made a fabulous lunch of chicken salad sandwiches with a Mediterranean pasta salad. I put a couple of water bottles and Diet Pepsis into the cooler.

We planned to drive ten minutes to the landfill, dump our trash, and then head to Almaden Lake for a celebratory picnic.

After loading the truck and heading for the Guadalupe Rubbish Disposal Facility, we turned right onto Guadalupe Mines Road. The line of cars going up the hill was like the end of *Field of Dreams*. "If they want to get rid of it, they will come," I said wryly.

"Should we come back another time?" Betsy asked.

"We've got Joe's truck loaded with garbage. I don't care how long this takes. We are getting rid of this truckload today."

We pulled up to the booth twenty-five minutes later. The garbage guy looked at our load and said, "That'll be $175."

I handed him cash, and he pointed up the hill. We drove through filthy dump dust toward the disposal area and passed truckloads of waste being emptied, creating mountain ranges of trash.

A worker wearing a neon orange vest pointed toward the right. We veered right, parked, got out, and chucked our refuse through the air into a pile.

"Betsy, look at that." I turned toward the exit. The line to get out appeared like the line getting in. "We'll never get out of here."

It was well past lunchtime. We'd eaten breakfast at 4 a.m. and were hungry and thirsty. I had to eat right then or lie down and become part of that toxic wasteland, so I grabbed my lawn chair from the back seat and stuck it on the grossest ground I'd ever sat on. Because piles of stinky debris surrounded me, I tried to concentrate on the magnificent backdrop of the Santa Cruz Mountains. Betsy sat in the truck with the windows closed.

I experienced a similar aroma as a kid when our family drove from Long Island to visit Uncle George and Aunt Joan in Princeton, New Jersey. After passing over the Verrazano Bridge from Brooklyn into Staten Island, the Goethals Bridge took us to Jersey City. A combination of sulfur, low tide, and fresh, stinky sewage sludge made a stench so pungent that even with the car windows closed, we held our breaths in disgust.

I didn't care. I was on a Hannah high. I picnicked right in the middle of the Guadalupe Landfill garbage dump.

"May we tailgate with you guys?" a gentleman asked, laughing after braking to stop.

"Sure, but we're wrapping this up as soon as the game starts."

His wife, Diane, got in the truck and sat with Betsy. I took out the other fold-up chair for Jack, and together we dined like rubbish royalty while talking sports and Hannah.

Jack lifted his Diet Pepsi. "A toast to Hannah."

A dump executive drove up and said, "Well, now I've seen everything." He shook his head.

"When we noticed the line of cars waiting to exit, we had to eat now or pass out." I offered him a plate of food, which he politely declined.

"I'm so sorry. A pile of trash collapsed. We had to close the exit while clearing a path." He handed us each one-hundred-dollar refund coupons and free tickets to a Giants game. The dump had season tickets.

"Thanks so much. You didn't have to," I said, grasping our undeserved prizes.

He raised his walkie-talkie to his mouth. "All clear." Then he pointed toward the exit. "I've got to go. Please come back soon." He gave a thumbs-up as his company vehicle roared off through rubbly roads into the land of refuse.

I looked toward the exit. The line of cars was gone. Betsy and I said goodbye to Jack and Diane and drove through the gate, down the hill, past the lake, and right to the house.

Betsy hurried inside as I stopped to admire the garage. It felt good to stand among such cleanliness. "Honey, it's spotless," I shouted. "We should have dinner out here."

"First, let me prepare the divorce papers," Betsy yelled.

I chuckled and went inside to remove my dirt-defiled clothing. We each enjoyed cleansing showers. "I'm glad we didn't have to try to conceive Hannah at that garbage dump," I joked while toweling off.

9

FACING THE BIOPSY WITH FRIENDSHIP, GOLF, AND HUMOR

Jordan and I met in 1990. We hit it off immediately.

It was typical for me to befriend such a quirky, outspoken, personable, and creative gentleman. He became my unofficial Jewish mother, best friend, and mentor—the guru who taught me to be a better man.

He and I were scheduled to meet at Silver Creek Valley Country Club for a round of golf the day before my biopsy.

We'd both been bartering services with Silver Creek for several years. I produce videos, and Jordan takes photographs. In return, we enjoy complimentary golf at a fabulous private club —a ten-minute drive from home—nestled in a remarkable setting. Each hole blends seamlessly with the naturally rugged and hilly landscape, and there's an occasional gallery of wild turkeys.

After the long uphill ride to the ninth tee, we exited our golf carts and took in the spectacular view of Silicon Valley before hitting our tee shots.

We walked to the edge of the cliff. Jordan put his arm around my shoulders and pointed toward one of the most prosperous valleys on earth. He said, "Everybody down there is working, and we've got

Silver Creek Golf Course to ourselves." He looked at me and became serious. "Tell me about the biopsy."

"I'm on the golf course in the present with my buddy, cherishing the valley vista. The biopsy may change my life forever. I'm not overly concerned, and I'll deal with it tomorrow."

"I'm proud of the way you're handling this, Henn. I love your attitude. Always positive and comical. You've been through a lot, and you know I'm always here if you need anything."

I knew that was a fact. It comforted me and made me feel cared for. Golfing through utopia with my buddy in excellent weather was the best pre-biopsy medicine.

June 2, 2009

I entered Doctor Jack's office. "Will I be leaving today's appointment with my brain intact?" I asked Janey.

"You have a brain, Mr. Hennessy?"

"There's so much brain." I pointed to my lower extremity. "I'm not concerned about the biopsy removing a couple of little pieces."

We both laughed.

"Your cerebral matter is going to be fine, Mr. Hennessy."

Doctor Jack and a nurse arrived just in time not to hear us giggling. The nurse took me into an exam room, and she and another nurse began preparing for the procedure.

"What's the big deal about prostate cancer?" I asked Doctor Jack as he entered. "It's slow-moving, right?"

"Mr. Hennessy, many have heard it's a slow-moving, non-killing cancer due to incompetent and confusing media reports. Approximately thirty thousand men in this country die from prostate cancer each year. This is not something to take lightly."

"I'm not concerned. There's no history of cancer in my family. I exercise and eat healthily. I don't smoke and hardly drink."

"That doesn't matter with prostate cancer. There's no protocol and no known way to avoid it. The only link we have to prostate cancer is red meat and processed meat."

"The only link you've got is red meat? They need to start figuring this out because it doesn't sound acceptable."

"I agree, Mr. Hennessy. We'll eventually get there."

I nodded.

"I will be snipping twelve pieces off your prostate. Each will subsequently be biopsied. You'll feel a strong pinch with each snip."

It was game time. I was lying on my back. Doctor Jack asked me to turn over on my side, then inserted a small ultrasound device into my rectum. "This unit will create images of your prostate, which will help me guide the needle placement. Then I will insert the needle through the rectum wall and into the prostate."

"Ouch!" I said after the first nip and felt that same sensation eleven more times.

"We're done. You've handled that well. Great job, Mr. Hennessy."

"Thanks, coach. Will I be able to work out at the gym today?"

"Let's take at least a week off from the gymnasium. After that, if you feel up to it, then go for it."

"How long until we get results?"

"Janey will make a follow-up for five days from today. We'll see you then."

"Thank you, Doctor Jack."

I left the exam room and headed to the office.

"How are you feeling?" Janey asked.

"I feel just as smart as before the procedure."

"Is that right?"

I took out my phone and visited the calculator app. "One thousand two hundred and fifty times thirty-five," I said as I pressed the buttons, "equals forty-three thousand seven hundred and fifty."

"I'm confused," Janey said.

"If I were any less smart, I wouldn't have thought to use my calculator."

"Very clever, Mr. Hennessy. I believe you're now smarter."

"Janey, will you do me one favor before I leave?"

"Sure."

"Would you please have a great rest of the day?"

"Aw, thanks. I absolutely will. I hope you do, too. We'll see you next week with good news."

"Here's to good news." I gave two thumbs up and walked out of the office.

10

THE DIAGNOSIS

June 7, 2009

Betsy and I entered Doctor Jack's office. Typically, Janey and I would banter, including with the nurses. Today was different. "Please take a seat, Mr. and Mrs. Hennessy." Janey pointed at the seating area without looking at us. Neither did the other staff, purposely ignoring me.

The vibe felt like walking into a funeral home's chapel moments before the memorial service began. Folks sit patiently in complete silence.

Maybe Janey is mad at me, or Doctor Jack ordered her not to joke around anymore. Maybe this, maybe that. I always have humor inside me, but I had no desire to access it.

The nurse who normally took me into rooms one, two, or three escorted us into Doctor Jack's private office. "The doctor will be with you shortly." As she closed the door, her face seemed to say, "I'm so sorry that you're about to receive awful news."

The office was a plain, undecorated, dimly lit room. The massive, old wooden office desk and chair were likely medical school graduation gifts purchased in 1978. The walls were ugly olive green, and

Doctor Jack's college and medical school certificates and diplomas hung in Walgreens frames.

Not only did the ambiance and waiting in silence mentally torture me, but they also reeked of bad news.

Time moved slowly. We sat there for thirty-five minutes, listening to the loudest silence I'd ever heard. They might have soundproofed this room for such patient reviews. If we concentrated enough, we could hear an ant crawl on the other side of the room or the splat the tiny particles of earth and waste called dust make when falling onto the floor.

I had been hopeful and imagined Doctor Jack following his staff through the door with jovial Janey holding a tray of fresh vegetables and fruit while singing, "There's great news for the Hennessys. Let's all have a good time." After a short celebration, Betsy and I would head to the Los Alamitos Trail for a late afternoon walk.

The door finally opened. Betsy held my hand tightly, just as she had done after discovering an issue with conceiving Hannah.

"It's not good news," Doctor Jack said, walking briskly into the room and shaking his head. "It's prostate cancer." He sat down behind his desk. "A very aggressive prostate cancer. Some prostate cancers are slow-growing and have a Gleason score of six. Seven is a dangerous level. Unfortunately, you're mostly eights and nines."

The news hit me like a sudden storm on a clear day, leaving me stunned and disoriented—the shock of the unexpected diagnosis reverberated through the room. It was like walking out of the Houston airport in mid-August, and the unanticipated wall of sweltering humid air slammed into you.

I had no recollection of discussing anything Gleason with Doctor Jack. I'd never even heard of the Gleason score, a grading system used to evaluate the aggressiveness of prostate cancer. A score of seven or higher indicates a more aggressive form of the disease. This lack of understanding added to my initial confusion and fear.

"I didn't expect this," Doctor Jack said, nodding. "It's surprising, especially at your age. I'm very sorry, Mr. Hennessy."

The average age of diagnosis was the late sixties. I was fifty-two.

"Your pregnancy is a miracle," he said, looking at Betsy. "I've never seen anything like it."

"On deck is surgery. Your only chance is to step up to the plate and let us knock this cancer out of the ballpark. A radical prostatectomy removes the entire prostate gland and surrounding areas. I believe we'll get all of it."

My brain was too flustered to process that.

"Your attitude is crucial. Stay your positive, uplifting, and humorous self."

I heard, understood, and remembered.

He kept talking, going into detail about surgery and percentages. I didn't hear any of it.

There's no protocol leading up to receiving a life-changing cancer diagnosis. Physicians don't prepare you for bad news, probably because you must assume you'll get good news. The lack of a procedure manual to help figure out what to do next was a stark reminder of the uncertainty and fear that comes with a cancer diagnosis.

Betsy and I plodded toward our car like two listless, heartbroken lovers in a tear-jerker movie scene. The crane with the camera was positioned near the ground as the director yelled, "Roll film."

Our teary eyes were despondently glued to the ground as the crane rose above the action, and two doves flew through the shot. Betsy and I held hands and gradually strolled through the parking lot toward our car.

"They had hoped and prayed for the best," the narrator said, "but were presented with the worst news. Betsy could have led Chris to any car in that parking lot, opened the door, and he would have entered without noticing."

The car doors close. Fade to black, end of scene.

We sat for a moment in silence. I switched the radio to soft music and texted my five siblings in one thread. "Biopsy results. I am proud to introduce cancer into the Hennessy family. Please call tomorrow and cheer me up. I'll need it."

Betsy started to cry.

I hugged her tightly. "Here's the plan. We'll live our lives as usual and keep moving mentally and physically—working, exercising, eating, sleeping, praying, loving, and laughing. Nothing changes.

"Hannah will grow up with two healthy, strong, loving parents. God is telling me this right now. I feel it. We're going to beat this.

"Let's walk on the trail, enjoy a meal, shower, and chill out while watching TV. When we get tired, we'll go to bed and sleep fabulously while holding on to each other all night."

Betsy wiped her eyes and nodded.

"We'll continue with the same routine. On Monday, we'll both have a great day working our butts off, then clearing our heads while running at the gym, and then enjoying dinner together."

"I love you and your plan," Betsy agreed.

We walked, talked, and showered, just like we'd have done had the news been good. After a fabulous meal, we relaxed and watched TV reruns.

We lay down, and Betsy led us in prayer. "Dear God, thanks for a great walk and pleasant evening. Please carry us through this difficult time and allow the doctors to rid Chris of this cancer. Keep us upbeat and strong so we can be the best parents for Hannah, and give us the strength to live our lives as if there weren't any cancer. Be ready to hear us talking to you more than usual."

Betsy fell asleep quickly.

I got up and wrote in my journal. "I imagined the world would stop for me. 'Humanity cannot go on until Chris is cancer-free.' However, the universe won't abruptly halt for anyone or anything. My friends and family can't be expected to stop living their lives because of my health issue, and that's okay."

11

THE MORNING AFTER THE DIAGNOSIS

I awoke the following day after Betsy left for work. For the first couple of seconds, I had a short spell from not being fully awake and aware. The shadeless windows filled the room with glorious natural light. I felt energetic and ready for a new day. Then I remembered, and my spirit spiraled into a pit of gloom. A claustrophobic cloud stationed itself in my mind. *There's no escaping this nightmare. Aggressive prostate cancer is inside me. I'm a doomed man.*

I put on the same pair of jeans I'd worn seventeen days in a row and grabbed a T-shirt— not caring which wound up in my hand— brushed my teeth, laced up my track shoes, snagged the newspaper, and got out of the lonely house.

Deciding to head to the closest hangout, I drove to Starbucks Princeton Plaza, a half-mile from the house.

Several of my longtime coffeehouse buddies were sitting at the corner table. "Hennessy!" they yelled, almost in unison. Jeff, Big Joe, Will, Scott, Paul, and Jordan were in a caffeine-laden discussion. I purchased a grande drip and sat down with the guys. The warmth of their company, the familiar banter, and the shared laughter felt like a comforting blanket. At that moment, I realized the profound importance of these relationships in my life. Coffee, conversation, and male bonding were just what I needed.

Big Joe no longer loved his wife, even though she was crazy about him. Will loves his wife, but she stopped loving him. Scott loves his wife and a dozen other women, too. Paul has a high-paying desk job, but his boss is an idiot. Will has a low-paying construction job, and they treat everyone like family.

We were in the midst of the worst recession since the Great Depression.

"I was just laid off," Paul shared.

"Sadly, most conversations these days include a story about someone who got laid off," Jordan said. "I'm so sorry, Paul."

"The cops are moaning because the city wants to cut their salaries 10 percent," Jeff, who is self-employed like Jordan and me, said. "I'd take that reduction in a heartbeat."

So would Jordan and I. Our businesses were down more than 50 percent.

"I've got to head home and get some work done." Jordan's office was also in his home.

"Me too," I said. "You guys have a good day."

We exited just as a young woman was walking in. Jordan held the door. I looked at her and deadpanned, shaking my head in disbelief. "They ran out of coffee."

She halted, obviously stunned.

"All the Starbucks in Northern California are out. We're headed to San Louis Obispo." I threw my hands up.

She tried to talk but stopped, still in disbelief.

"Just kidding." I looked at her and smiled; I had never seen such a relieved look on a human face.

"You guys are hilarious." She laughed, realizing she'd been punked. "You got me good. I think I'll treat myself to a venti this morning."

"I believe you deserve a free venti today," Jordan said, slipping five dollars into her hand.

"Aw, thanks for brightening my day."

"I wonder how many people will hear her Starbucks story?" I asked Jordan as we walked toward our vehicles.

"It'll probably go viral in her community," he said, and we both laughed.

"Henn, I've been waiting on the biopsy results."

"Aggressive prostate cancer." I looked into his eyes. "They took twelve slices from my prostate, and every one had cancer."

"Oy. What's next?"

"Betsy and I haven't made up our minds. The options are surgery or radiation seeds."

Jordan hugged me. We held each other tightly right in the middle of the crowded Starbucks parking lot. He began to bawl. That made me cry. We both couldn't care less what anybody thought. "How's Betsy?"

"I told Betsy we will hold our heads high, continue living life as usual, and beat this."

"I'm proud of you, Henn. Your attitude blows me away. Keep trucking, man. I love you. Call me anytime. Talk to you later."

Instead of heading home and getting to work, I deviated from my usual post-coffeehouse routine, put on music, and drove to the foothills. There was no hurry to get back to the office. Screw the office. Livelihood was less crucial than smelling the roses.

It's fascinating how music can induce me into a zone of euphoria. Occasionally, I'll listen to the same song looped repeatedly for hours.

For an hour, I drove leisurely through the Santa Teresa Hills of South San José, serenading the neighborhood with Incubus's "Earth to Bella." I treasured the moments and inhaled the delicious draft, which brushed both sides of my face.

Paying special attention to the trees, I pondered how underrated they are. Many people barely notice their majestic presence. They stand tall and mighty, adding a picturesque ambiance to our hills and neighborhoods.

We drive by in our air-polluting vehicles, not noticing how trees help remove the filthy by-products from the atmosphere. We let our dogs urinate on them, and we might do the same after a few beers.

Like mail carriers, trees don't seek refuge during rain, sleet, or snowstorms. They provide shade on a sunny day and offer shelter to all living things while helping to reduce erosion and moderate the climate.

I stopped to admire the exquisite branches of a eucalyptus tree and enjoyed the sight and sound of leaves rustling in summer breezes.

I looked closely at one leaf, noticing its long, slender, oval shape. The leathery, waxy surface hides millions of extensively vascularized cells, more complex than any invented technology. They bring water and minerals from the roots into the leaf and increase the absorption of carbon dioxide. An eighty-five-foot-tall tree absorbs nearly fifty pounds of carbon dioxide and can produce almost six thousand pounds of oxygen yearly, enough to support at least two people.

After my little excursion, I had a new respect for trees and the many miracles within one life. I'd elevated myself from the darkness of the cancer diagnosis and returned to the office, ready to accomplish work.

Chatting with my parents and five siblings that afternoon lifted me. My brother Russ, a lieutenant in the Nassau County NYPD, gave me a very inspiring talk.

"Stand up like the man you are. This is war, and you're going to win this battle. I love you, and I've always looked up to you, Keek"—my nickname since we were toddlers—"I know you can beat this."

My special folks are three thousand miles away. I wish we could be closer.

After a productive afternoon in the office, I ran for thirty-five minutes at the gym on the elliptical with my headphones delivering spirited music. By the time Betsy and I hooked up for dinner, I'd had a day filled with energetic mental and physical activity.

That night, I wrote this in my journal:

Come to think of it, we're insignificant. We live on an amusement park-like ride called Earth, spinning steadily, circling our star faithfully. That's how we measure time.

Our planet is merely a grain of sand among billions of galaxies.

But this place is fascinating. Trees, soil, air, mountains, oceans, and plenty of life exist. Everything we know is held together by gravity. Without it, the brilliant teal-blue sky and cotton candy clouds would be sucked up instantly, disappearing forever into the endless black vacuum of space.

The sun bombards us with nourishing solar energy all day long. Darkness spreads like the San Francisco fog and its thick, cozy blanket of micro-tiny pristine water droplets, climbing the Golden Gate Bridge at night, covering everything in its path.

Stars and distant galaxies appear in the nighttime sky. This is the perfect scenario for us to sleep unconscious so our trillions of cells can be re-energized and ready for tomorrow. As we lie sleeping, our solar system drifts endlessly through the infinite nothing of space.

It makes me realize that nobody, or anything, is so essential to be taken too seriously except our relationships with loved ones.

The life-threatening pressure motivated me to perform at a higher, more productive, and creative level for the next several months. Staying active and not sitting around sulking helped me to thrive. I cranked out some of the best video work of my career.

12

MY MEDICAL GUARDIAN ANGEL

Receiving a cancer diagnosis can lead to a whirlwind of emotions. The initial shock and confusion can be overwhelming, leaving one unsure of which direction to head. Positive thoughts can quickly twist into knots of negativity, a common experience in this journey.

Post-diagnosis, it's like trying to build a house without any knowledge of construction. This is where a competent general contractor becomes necessary.

When diagnosed with cancer, we must become our own general contractors. It's challenging, especially for those who have never studied medicine or worked in the medical field. But it's a role we must embrace to navigate the journey.

I realized I needed more guidance than Doctor Jack provided, and remembered Doctor Amir Saffarian, my upcoming wedding client, was a urologist.

Aida Mohsenin and Amir Saffarian were to be married on June 27, 2009, at Silver Creek Valley Country Club. We'd met for an initial consultation in January 2009 and immediately hit it off. They were a classy, fun, and personable couple, and I felt a strong sense of camaraderie with them. Amir's expertise and understanding would be invaluable in my journey. With determination, I reached out for his support.

I called Aida and explained my situation. She gave me Amir's cell number. I left Amir a voicemail, and he called back within minutes.

"Thanks so much for calling, Amir."

"It's my pleasure, Chris. How can I be of help?"

"I was recently diagnosed with prostate cancer and was wondering if you could help me proceed." I provided details about my condition, including dates, blood tests, and Gleason scores.

"This is a serious cancer. You need to seek a prostate cancer specialist. I'll send you several links to articles that will help you get up to speed on what you're dealing with."

"Perfect. Betsy, her parents, and I are headed to Carmel Valley on Friday morning for a weekend getaway. I'll have plenty of time to read and study the pieces."

"I'd like to see and discuss your full biopsy report," Amir said. "Aida and I are having lunch on Friday at the Highlands Inn in Carmel. We'll celebrate and reminisce at that wonderful location where we had our first date. Can you meet up with your biopsy report for a short consultation?"

"Good for you guys. That sounds like a grand afternoon, and the timing is excellent. We're arriving around noon. I'll get us checked in and settled at the hotel and then head to the restaurant."

I continued, "I'd like to return the favor. I propose that we film you and Aida at the Highlands. I'll craft a short film from the footage that we could feature at the reception on a big screen."

"That's unnecessary, but I love it, and Aida will too."

"You two will be fabulous. It'll be a blast."

"From the parking area, walk toward the main building," he said. "We'll be at the flagpole, where Aida and I first met. We reserved the same table where we dined on our first date."

Highlands Inn overlooks some of the most stunning ocean vistas on the Big Sur coastline. I planned to recreate the look and atmosphere of their first date and then edit something exceptional for them to cherish forever.

Betsy and I were excited as we prepared to introduce Carmel Valley to her parents. Their presence and support would enrich our journey and add a layer of anticipation.

With Mom and Dad driving down from Davis to our place in San José, we were all set for the journey. We comfortably loaded into Betsy's SUV, and I took the wheel for the one-and-a-half-hour drive to the Monterey Peninsula. As we traveled, we chatted and laughed with country music playing in the background. Our conversation turned to awe an hour into the trip when we exited onto the scenic California State Route 1, with the Pacific Ocean and its deep blue waters, brilliant white sands, and seagulls patrolling for food, painting a breathtaking panorama.

Passing the turnoff for Carmel-by-the-Sea, the small beach town we'd visit during our stay, we turned east onto Carmel Valley Road, which winds twelve miles inland through tucked-away inns and lodges, fields of organic vegetables, vineyards, championship golf courses, and award-winning restaurants to Carmel Valley Village. Carmel Valley Lodge was well hidden below the road just before the village.

Betsy and I unpacked inside our favorite room. Mom and Dad were in the adjoining room. We met them on our connected patios and peered at a spectacular view of palm trees, a pool, and the Santa Lucia Mountains.

"Goodbye, sweet family. I'll be back in a couple of hours."

"We love you. We'll be praying," Betsy's mom said.

"This is nerve-wracking," I told Betsy as she walked me to the car.

"I understand. I'd be happy to join you."

"No, please stay with your parents and enjoy this ambiance. I'll do my thing and be back soon."

"We trust Amir. You're in good hands. Please be safe. I love you."

"Love you, too."

I drove twenty minutes through the narrow Carmel Valley toward the coast, with jagged mountains on both sides funneling refreshing Pacific Ocean air into my open windows like a natural air conditioner.

I parked and trudged with my video camera and tripod up a winding hill through the parking lot. With a breathtaking backdrop sketched behind them, the two lovers stood by the flagpole.

We hugged and chatted. Amir asked to see my biopsy report. His eyes opened wide, and he focused, taking a few minutes to read and understand my fate.

"This is very significant stuff," he said, looking at me. "I've never seen such a biopsy. You have unusually aggressive prostate cancer. A radical prostatectomy to remove the prostate and surrounding tissue is your only shot at surviving.

"Getting the operation accomplished ASAP could be the difference between life and death. Hopefully, the cancer hasn't spread outside the prostate. If it has, this could be what kills you."

A dreadful, helpless feeling surged through me. "One doctor mentioned that planting radiation seeds throughout the area instead of surgery was the best option."

"I believe the cancer would march right through those seeds and out of the prostate," he said. "Remember, this isn't ordinary prostate cancer. It's faster moving and destructive."

"I understand. I've identified Doctor Preston Peterkin, a prostate cancer specialist at Stanford who's done many radical prostatectomies. I've confirmed that my insurance will cover it."

"Great job. Now, book a consultation with Doctor Peterkin, and then book the surgery. Get it done."

"I will on Monday. Now, it's time to have some fun," I said, forcing a smile and holding my head high, even though I felt like crumbling.

We walked to the entrance and stopped. With a backdrop of blue and purple foliage, colorful roses, California cypress trees, and the Pacific Ocean, I interviewed the couple about the happiest occasion of their lives amidst the most awful moments of mine.

"What was going through your head when you arrived, Amir?"

"Well, I was hoping Aida would show up."

We laughed.

"When she appeared, it was the most stunning sight ever. There were no nerves—she was so easy to be around and talk to. We've been inseparable ever since."

"Aida, was there a first kiss on that date?"

"Oh yes, there was," she said, smiling at Amir. "We looked at each other on the beach and instinctively kissed, naturally and romantically."

"Was it love at first date?"

"Yes!" both said without hesitation.

I secured romantic cutaway shots at their table from every imaginable angle—they were toasting, chuckling, chatting, and kissing. After lunch, we recreated shots of their first kiss at the beach and returned to the parking area.

"Remaining healthy, upbeat, and strong will get you through this," Amir said as we hugged. "I'm proud of everything you've done to get to this point. I'm ordering you to have a fabulous weekend with your family. Thanks for coming out. We'll see you in a couple of weeks."

"Thanks to both of you for your love and support. It means—"

Amir cut me off, looked into my eyes, and said, "I'm here for you, always."

I gave a thumbs-up, turned around, walked to the car, randomly placed my equipment on the back seat, and drove back to Betsy.

Doctor Amir's consultation provided comfort. Having a knowledgeable ally in this battle was immense. He became my mentor and friend, always taking the time to listen, offer advice, and push me to act.

I couldn't appreciate music or scenery while navigating one of Earth's most gorgeous valleys. I didn't notice the scent of freshly cut lawns and trimmed flowers in the hotel parking area. Our room was empty, but I saw the family lounging at the pool through the sliding glass doors. I went to them to share Doctor Amir's explanation of my biopsy. Normally, it took a lot for me to shed tears; however, this was not a normal time. I put my head down and sobbed.

Betsy placed her soft arm around me. Dad asked us to hold hands and led a prayer. "Father God, thank you for providing Chris with

Amir, his guardian angel. Please keep a loving hand on Chris and help him and Betsy through this voyage. We pray that the surgery completely eradicates the cancer."

A peaceful, post-bawling feeling replaced the dread. My family's love and support consoled me and lifted my spirits, as did my guardian angel's. *Everything is going to be okay.*

"Let's head to the rooms and get freshened up for dinner," Betsy said. "Mom and Dad, we'll meet you at the parking area in twenty minutes."

We walked a short way to the village, had a fabulous dinner, and then enjoyed being together for the entire weekend. I forgot the cancer and lived as usual, just as the doctor ordered.

13

SERVING IN CHILDREN'S MINISTRY

Betsy and I have regularly attended the vibrant Westgate Church since 2005. In 2007, we felt a calling to contribute more actively, and our involvement in the children's ministry significantly enhanced our community church experience.

"They're looking for children's ministry helpers to care for kids while their parents attend service," Betsy said.

"That sounds like a good opportunity."

She signed us up to lead a class.

Our first assignment was a group called walkers—toddlers who'd recently started walking—during the 9:30 a.m. service.

Debbie, the children's ministry leader, brought us into the fish room, a brightly decorated space with fish-themed murals. It had a large play area with plenty of toys, books on shelves, and a table and chairs for snack time.

"Thanks for being here. Here's your pager. Reach out if needed. Be patient and have fun."

About fifteen minutes before service begins, the KidzTown building bustles with family energy. Parents leave their children in age-appropriate rooms and head to the main sanctuary.

Betsy and I stood at the fish room door, savoring the lively atmosphere. Kaylee's mom approached and looked at us. I stepped forward, and she placed her little blonde walker into my arms, turned around, and left. It was an instant connection. I confidently put Kaylee's crying, precious head onto my shoulder, walked to the shelves, picked up a doll, and handed it to her. She grabbed dolly and held on firmly to both of us.

"Kaylee," I said softly, "Miss Betsy and I love you very much. We will care for you while your mom and dad are in the church service. They're learning about God."

She continued to bawl.

"Kaylee, it's beautiful outside." I walked to the window and pointed. "God gave us a sunny, beautiful day." I turned around. "The kids are playing and having fun. Soon, we'll enjoy a yummy snack." I showed her the little salted fish crackers. "Do you like these?"

She nodded, expressionless, and the colossal sobbing turned into softer weeping.

"Then we'll go outside and play. Would you like to play at the park?"

She nodded with her eyes opening wider.

I was excited to be winning her over. Crying was now history. She looked at the other kids who were enjoying the toys and games. "Let me know when you're ready to get down and play." Soon, she wiggled from my arms. I placed her on the floor, and off she went into playland.

"Ethan, these are your new leaders, Chris and Betsy," Dana said as she handed me her son Ethan. "Hey Chris, this is my husband, Peter, and I'm Dana. Ethan, please behave and have a great time."

"He's in good hands, Momma," I said.

They turned, held hands, and strolled away on their Sunday morning date as tears cascaded from Ethan's eyes.

I talked to Ethan as I had spoken to Kaylee. His crying quickly turned to laughter, but the tears kept flowing. He repeated the precious sight weekly. Soon, he'd join the others in the play area, and I'd return to the door, ready for my next challenge.

"We've tried several churches, and none has been able to handle

Nicholas," Nicholas's mom said after checking us out from the back of the room.

We'll see about that. I pried Nicholas from his mom's arms. She walked out of the room, and Nicholas screeched. As I'd done with Kaylee and Ethan, I carried him and talked patiently to him. Twenty minutes later, he was still crying and screaming.

But I didn't give up. Giving up meant paging Debbie. During service, Nicholas's number would appear on the big screen, notifying his parents to retrieve him. I didn't want to disrupt the parents, so I kept smiling, walking, and talking tenderly about the paintings on the walls, the games to play, the weather, and anything else I could think of.

Finally, about an hour after being dropped off, there were only post-crying sniffles. I put Nicholas down, but he'd only play if I remained at his side.

The shrieking and weeping lessened weekly and eventually stopped. He stayed close and played—frequently peering at me with big brown eyes beaming as if to say, "I'm good, Mr. Chris, as long as you're here with me."

The kids enjoyed climbing up and sliding down our small plastic slide. I kneeled at the bottom and snatched each one after gliding down. "One two, buckle my shoe!" I counted, then carefully threw each up in the air, catching them on the way down.

The class lined up for their free ride on the slide and then up into the air. Over and over, kid after kid. "One two, buckle my shoe!"

The room suddenly filled with a foul smell. Betsy went from child to child, sniffing diapers. She lifted her head from Emma's bottom. "Yup, it's Emma."

From then on, I called Emma Poop-Dee-Doo.

When Betsy sang "Snack Time" at 10:15 a.m., the children eagerly echoed her, their eyes lighting up with excitement. Their enthusiasm for snack time became a small but significant part of our weekly routine. This shared experience fostered a strong sense of community and togetherness.

Charlotte dragged a six-foot stuffed horse to the table. "Hi, kids, it's me, Mr. Horsey," I said while holding Horsey. "Are you hungry and ready for a snack?"

"Yes!" they shouted.

"First, I will lead us in prayer. 'God, thanks for the food you've provided and the delicious water, which is much healthier than soda. Thanks for our pastor, who teaches Mommy and Daddy about you. Please make it a fabulous day and week for all the kids and their families. Amen.'

"Amen! Amen! Amen!" I said while pounding on the table with both clenched fists. With each bash, we'd all shout several times, "Amen! Amen! Amen!"

Then, I told a story while Betsy set the table with napkins, snacks, and water. Instead of reading the text, I held Mr. Horsey before me and ad-libbed a story, showing the pictures and making up a fun, inspiring tale. Improv storytelling became a snack-time ritual.

At the end of our first class, Eric and Jamie Montoya sauntered into the room, astonished to witness Kaylee playing so happily.

"This was our first time experiencing an entire service together. Thank you two so much."

"Kaylee stopped crying after a few minutes and then stayed busy playing. She's awesome. We had a blast and can't wait to see her next week."

The Montoyas smiled, hugged Kaylee, had her wave bye, and left.

Children's ministry became the most enjoyable and rewarding activity Betsy and I did together. We discovered that it was possible to make friends with people who were not quite two years old, most with little vocabulary. Kids who can't yet speak understand much more than most people realize.

After we served, Betsy and I relaxed and enjoyed the 11 a.m. service.

We developed close friendships with the Montoyas, several other parents, and their children. Soon, families lined up at the fish room door early to get their children into our class before it filled.

When the last Sunday in October arrived, Betsy said, "Our three-month shift is over after today. We take a three-month break and then return for three more months."

Sunday mornings without Kaylee, Ethan, Charlotte, Nicholas, Nathanial, and Poop-Dee-Doo didn't feel right. "Do we have to take a three-month break?"

"I have no idea. Let's page Debbie."

Probably thinking there was an issue, Debbie showed up within seconds.

"Debbie, do we have to take a three-month break?"

"No, of course not." Her face brightened. "The children thrive with consistent care providers."

"Sweet," I said, relieved. "We'll see you next week."

14

SURGERY WEEK: LIVING LIFE AS USUAL

June 2009

Five of six prostate cancer specialists agreed with Amir that my only chance of surviving was to undergo a radical prostatectomy to remove my prostate and the surrounding tissue.

I booked an appointment with Doctor Preston Peterkin at Stanford University Cancer Center, a highly regarded prostate cancer specialist who'd performed dozens of radical prostatectomies.

After driving for half an hour, I turned right and down the ramp into the Stanford Hospital underground garage. On the first try, I aced a parallel park. Then I closed the windows, turned off the radio, and chuckled while exiting the car. *I'm going to tell everyone I'm attending Stanford.*

I walked up two flights of stairs and outside, past the elevators, into the sun-kissed campus. I noticed a small crowd waiting for the shuttle. I decided to walk three-quarters of a mile through the bustling but beautiful Stanford University grounds. Fifteen minutes of movement in wonderful weather eased everything. When I arrived at my location, the automatic glass doors opened, and I sauntered into a new, unfamiliar world. *What am I doing here?*

Before me were three front desks, shielded with glass. "Please take a seat, Mr. Hennessy," the receptionist said after taking my information.

Minutes later, a nurse entered the waiting area. "Chris Hennessy," she called out while looking down at her notes. I stood and moved toward her. "Welcome, Mr. Hennessy. Please follow me to exam room E." She smiled, turned, walked through the hallway, and then took a left into the room. "Please take a seat. I'm going to conduct five tests."

"What is it like working with Doctor Peterkin?" I asked.

"He's a brilliant gentleman and the most competent doctor I've worked with. Patients and staff love and respect him."

"Thanks so much." I'd interviewed thousands on camera and knew hers was an authentic testimonial.

Ten minutes later, she said, "I've completed all the tests. Doctor Pee Pee will be in shortly."

"Ma'am, this is my first appointment." I chuckled. "I have no idea who Doctor Pee Pee is."

"Doctor Preston Peterkin," she said, grinned, then turned around and left.

I laughed again. *I'm cracking up during the most consequential appointment of my life. Perfect.*

Doctor Peterkin arrived, and I said, "The nurse told me they call you Doctor Poo Poo."

"Pee Pee, Poo Poo. Maybe I should be in pediatrics?"

I laughed.

Doctor Peterkin was confident, caring, personable, and professional, with a quick-witted sense of humor. I trusted him and scheduled surgery for August 3, 2009.

I let go of my problems when I left Doctor Peterkin's office and headed to film a Zumba promotional video for a local sports and fitness center. Staying busy doing what I enjoyed—directing, filming, and editing gigs like that—was what my soul and I needed.

"Are you guys ready for Zumba?" I climbed on stage, grabbed the mic, yelled, and pumped my fist. The uproarious cheer showed they were into it and ready.

"I'll be weaving through and filming with a handheld camera. Keep doing your thing as if I weren't there."

High-volume Latin-inspired music jetted at the speed of sound from the two giant speakers on stage. "Let's make this the best class ever!" They erupted into a raucous roar as I leaped into Zumbaville. Seventy-five ready-to-kick-some-butt Zumba dancers started twisting, swaying, bopping, and hopping.

A random body thrust herself before the camera and slithered like an exotic dancer performing acrobatic tricks on a pole. She ripped off her shirt. My lens thought it was getting an X-rated performance, but our burlesque queen wore a sports bra.

We fist-bumped, and I randomly handed her the camera. She pointed it at me. I grasped my T-shirt, tore it off, peered into the camera, flexed my right bicep, and threw that 100 percent cotton cloth into Zumba land. Their earsplitting response and knowing I was getting excellent footage made me feel like a movie star. It was another typical day at the office.

My five-minute Zumba video became an early YouTube hit, garnering over two million views in its first year. Thousands watched daily, making it one of the viral videos that helped bring Zumba to the forefront of aerobic exercise.

The days in the week leading up to surgery could have been miserable and filled with anxiety and stress. They were the total opposite. I lived life as usual through August 3, immersing myself in activities I'm passionate about. I visited coffee joints and socialized each morning. I returned to the office, worked on client video projects through the afternoon, and ran forty minutes daily on the elliptical while listening to uplifting music.

Betsy and I enjoyed dinners and conversations together, and then

I headed into my office and worked on a video that would tell the story of my life. I acquired photos, videos, and film footage of myself and my family dating back to the late 1950s and completely immersed myself in the project. I couldn't wait to get in front of my computer to continue crafting my masterpiece.

Each evening, a confident attitude without issues, problems, worries, or fears boosted me while keeping my mind present and in the moment. Staying focused and the ensuing natural high caused my creativity to spill out.

I meticulously sliced, diced, and crafted a five-minute film titled "Recent Random Thoughts." I was proud of my work, and it made for a fulfilling, memorable week.

It was August 2, the day before surgery, and someone suggested we take the day off from our children's ministry duties at church. I'm so glad we didn't follow that advice. Nothing we could've done that day would have been more gratifying than being around the kids and their families.

As parents arrived from the service to retrieve their kids, they gave hugs, cards, balloons, and prayers. I felt like James Stewart at the end of *It's a Wonderful Life.* Those people cared and promised prayers for me that night, the next night, and beyond. They made sure God got an earful.

Nicholas and his parents were the last to say goodbye. "You've done so much for our son, and now God is sending you away from us," his dad said.

"God is sending me to be healed, and then I'll be back stronger than ever. Nicholas has adjusted to class, and he'll be fine." I picked him up, hugged him long and hard, and said, "I love you, Nicholas."

"Chris, we love you and will constantly pray for you. Thanks so much for everything," Nicholas's misty-eyed mom said. She then turned, took Nicholas from me, and they left.

I looked out the window and watched them walk toward the

parking lot. The dad stopped and looked back. The pained look on his face told a story of sadness and concern that I'd never witnessed, and it touched me deeply.

Betsy and I walked out of the fish room, and Betsy gasped. We had yet to notice that parents and kids congregated in the courtyard. I looked up, stunned to see a hundred people or more.

Lizzy, head pastor of the children's ministry, asked for quiet. "Father God, thank you so much for bringing Chris and Betsy to our Westgate community. This lovely and devoted family is now in your hands." She looked at us and continued, "Please lift them and help them persevere and come out of this healthy, strong, cancer-free, and back to us soon."

The crowd remained silent, many wiping tears, and then people greeted us, forming an impromptu receiving line. We hung out for an hour, having a grand time chatting with good folks.

"That outpouring of support has me on top of the world," I told Betsy.

Betsy nodded. "What a blessing that we found Westgate."

Chilling out and watching Wimbledon and reruns on TV with my pregnant wife made for a delightful evening. The last thing I wanted to do was change our routine.

15

RADICAL PROSTATECTOMY CANCER SURGERY

August 3, 2009

"You won't sleep well the night before surgery," my mom warned me.

Betsy and I lay down at 10 p.m., and I quickly went unconscious. I awoke at 6 a.m. after eight hours of deep sleep. My gorgeous wife's eyes slowly opened. "Bets, that was the best sleep I've had since I can remember. I feel great."

"That's amazing." Her eyes opened wide.

"I feel completely rested." My hibernation session had me rein-vigorated, unafraid, and ready. "Caring moms aren't always right on with their advice."

"Your mom is still tied with my mom as the best mom ever."

"Agreed. Thanks, Bets."

Being in Betsy's presence aroused my animalistic desires. I wanted and needed her right then, which was typical on most mornings. I leaned over, and we kissed. She pulled me down under the covers, and then I caressed and chewed lightly on her volup-tuous shoulders, leading to a vigorous pre-surgery love-making session. The intercourse of our bodies in rhythm as one was like every instrument in the symphony playing in unison, then the piece peaks loudly, brilliantly, and beautifully. The audience's hunger for entertainment was satisfied, as were Betsy's and my need for each other.

I'd done my homework and acknowledged that surgery could bring an end to our sex life. Only time would tell if we'd just experienced our last love-making session. If the ability hadn't returned within a year, then a chunk of my manhood would be gone for good.

"Honey, I'm starved. What's for breakfast?" I asked and walked out of the bedroom, knowing I couldn't eat that morning.

"I'm sorry, but the kitchen's closed," Betsy yelled from the bathroom.

I was dressed, and Betsy was still getting ready when Harrison and Hendrix arrived on time—a minor miracle. It was great to have my two big, handsome sons support me.

The four of us chatted as if we were on a family outing and arrived at Stanford Hospital's admission desk at 9 a.m. on August 3, 2009. "I admit that I'm supposed to be at Admitting being admitted for surgery," I said to the receptionist.

"I see our pre-surgery tutorial helped," she said, chuckling. "May I have your name and birthdate?"

"Chris Hennessy. February 24, 1957."

"Mr. Hennessy, we're going to take excellent care of you."

"That's very sweet. Thank you." I turned to my sons and said, "Please make a note to send her a bottle of fine Hennessy Cognac." I turned to the receptionist, and her face gleamed as if she believed I was associated with Hennessy Cognac. We fist-bumped.

Shortly after we took our seats in the waiting room, a nurse arrived and called, "Chris Hennessy." I stood up. "Good morning, Mr. Hennessy. We're going that way." She pointed, and the four of us followed her to the surgery waiting area, where she handed me a surgical gown and closed the cubicle curtain. Before walking away, she said, "Please put this on. They'll be back to get you in about fifteen minutes."

"I can never negotiate this stupid piece of fabric," I said with one arm in front and the other behind me, obviously in the wrong armholes. "It's open in the back and closed in the front. Am I supposed to have my butt exposed?"

"Let me help you," Betsy said, and helped me quickly put on the gown and lie down.

Betsy's parents arrived, followed by Jordan and several church friends, filling our area with jovial chatting.

"Hey guys"—they quieted as I spoke—"thanks so much for coming out to support a brother." The group of fifteen cheered as if they were a crowd of one hundred fifteen. "Your love and support will help Betsy, Hannah, and me through this," I said, clasping my hands together as if praying. "I'm confident we're going to eradicate this disease. Cancer is going down." They hollered and applauded. "I've already survived the most difficult part." I sat up, turned around, and said, "Putting on this silly reverse gown." They laughed as if I'd delivered the best punchline of the night at San José Improv.

Doctor Peterkin walked in and said, "This is unprecedented pre-surgery behavior." He shook his head. Our startled group assumed we were getting a lecture on waiting room behavior. "I love it!" Doctor Peterkin exclaimed, and they cheered. He looked at me and said, "Good for you, Chris. I'm proud to be here."

"We're blessed to have you, Doctor Pee Pee," I said, addressing my audience. "Doctor Peterkin will give autographs in the lobby after saving my life." I grabbed my gown. "The signed gown will be mine."

Doctor Peterkin's smile then became straight-faced. "We're about ready to bring Chris to surgery. Feel free to take a couple of minutes and say your goodbyes." He looked at me. "I'll see you in a few minutes." He gave a thumbs-up, nodded, turned to the others, and pointed to the left. "The surgery waiting area is just up the hall," he said, walking out.

"Father God, please keep this unruly crowd away from the coffee and donuts." I paused and closed my eyes. "Give Doctor Peterkin his A-game focus and ability to remove all cancer. Please watch over Betsy and Hannah and allow us to be a loving family together."

Betsy, her parents, my two sons, and Jordan stayed with me. Two male nurses arrived.

"It's time to take Chris," one of the nurses said. He came to the front of my bed, the other nurse went behind, and they wheeled me away.

"Wait," Betsy cried out, grabbing for me. She reached down, hugged me, and kissed my cheek, pushing flesh deep into my bone and giving me chills. "I love you," she said through her tears.

"There's no crying in surgery," I deadpanned, providing comic relief. The nurses smiled. "I love you, Bets." I was teary-eyed myself as they pushed me toward the door.

As I'd always asked the guy in the clubhouse before every round of golf, I looked back at Jordan and asked, "Is it okay if we par the first hole?"

"Henn, you're going to birdie it," he answered.

Betsy threw a kiss, and then my bed and I entered the surgery area, with the doors closing behind us. *I cannot believe this is happening.*

The anesthesiologist asked me to lie still and began the process of hooking the anesthetic into my IV line. I noticed a ray of sunlight on the ceiling near the harsh, cold fluorescent light.

The ceiling seemed to be painted in deep, vivid colors—yellow, orange, red—with a warm, film-look richness, especially when compared to the video-like yellow and whites from fluorescent light, which is fine fake light for corporate cubicles, kitchens, and hospital hallways. I was glad I never had to work in such an environment.

"I'm going to have you count backward from one hundred," the anesthesiologist said.

"This morning, we'll make it a bit more challenging."

As my puzzled anesthesiologist was about to speak, I began slowly counting backward. "One million. Nine hundred thousand, nine hundred ninety-nine. Nine hundred thousand, nine hundred ninety-eight. Nine-hundred thousand, nine hundred ninety-sev—"

The master of manual dexterity is what experts in the Stanford community called Doctor Peterkin. His long, elegant, soft but powerful hands and nimble fingers began doing their thing.

Doctor Peterkin's sanitized surgery knife made a retropubic slash from right below my navel down to the pubic region. If cancerous tissue were tangled with the nearby bundle of nerves, the nerves would have to be cut and the surrounding lymph nodes removed. That would not be good news for our sex life.

I lay on the operating table, unaware. Because nerves can't pass signals to the brain, I didn't feel anything under anesthesia, and there was no passage of time.

Betsy filled me in on her waiting experience later.

"Thank God you had me anticipating only good news—and my parents, Jordan, Harrison, and Hendrix were there to help me pass the time. We had lunch in the cafeteria," she said. "I could barely eat. Hendrix finished my leftovers, and then we ambled to the waiting room, which was a true test of my stamina and sanity.

I was about to put my head back down when the door opened for the hundredth time, and Doctor Peterkin approached with a slight grin.

"The surgery went as well as we'd hoped," he told me. "Chris is doing fine in the recovery area. It'll be about half an hour before we can let you in. I believe we got it all, but I will know when the pathology report is issued in three to five days."

My beautiful wife recalled how she had so much pent-up tension, she knew she had to let go of it. "Healing tears finally poured like a cleansing summer rain from my eyes," she said. "Crying long and hard was like taking a heavy weight off my back."

Eventually, after a lengthy, distressing wait, a medical team member escorted Betsy and her parents to my side. "Pops, you are the best dad and father-in-law. We love you," I repeatedly told Dad while under the influence of powerful painkillers. I pushed the morphine button as allowed every two minutes, and my mind couldn't fully control what my mouth spewed out.

My brain added words to a tune it thought up. "Life is keen on morphine—do you know what I mean? I've seen the scene, dreamed the dream. I pushed on the button, and it gave me more morphine."

When my talking became mostly muttering with eyes closed, Betsy knew it was time to say goodbye and let me rest in the care of Stanford Hospital, unit C-2.

16

"HOLD ON!" CODE BLUE MOMENT

At 2 a.m., I opened my eyes, and two nurses were at work on my IV line, likely making sure I remained drugged up like a junkie. I felt moderate pain yet was miserable knowing it was only because of the narcotics that the postoperative, acute-ten pain didn't torment me.

After flesh and tissue had been slashed, my entire inner being was in what-the-heck-happened mode. My nervous system got information from my body and sent code-red distress messages: "There's been a major attack with severe injury to the abdomen. There may not be enough platelets to help your skewered wound. Send all back-ups at once." My brain acknowledged the agonizing pain and swelling and delivered everything I had within me to fight my battle.

The day after surgery, I awoke at 7 a.m. feeling lousy and wanting to be home with Betsy. A nurse stood beside my bed, fiddling with the drip.

"Have you been standing there all night?" I mumbled.

"No, sir. I just walked in, and I'm getting your vitals," she said and smiled.

"Please don't call me sir," I whispered and breathed. "Call me Uncle Sir."

"Why Uncle Sir?"

"I don't want you to call me Aunt Sir." I mustered a chuckle. Her bewildered look and chortle satisfied my need to confuse and spawn laughter.

"Well, anyway, I'm happy to be your nurse today. I'm Beth."

"Hi, Beth. I'm Chris, and I'm famished." I hadn't eaten in thirty-six hours.

"Unfortunately, you'll have to stay hungry for now."

"Do you know when they'll let me eat?"

"You'll get a freshly cooked hospital meal for dinner the day after tomorrow."

"I'm in the hospital? I thought this was heaven."

"I don't believe heaven serves hospital food," Beth said. She and I chuckled.

"Our back-and-forth banter helped my brain to function. What's next?"

"I'm going to help you get up and take a short walk."

"I can walk? They said I'd never walk again." I acted out and flexed my right bicep. "Let's do this, Beth."

"The more walking at this point, the better."

"I understand." I slowly stood with Beth's help, put one foot in front of the other, and walked out of my room and into the hall. "That wasn't as tough as I thought it would be."

"I'm proud of you, Chris. This is a good sign."

I sauntered twenty yards up and back.

"Good job. We'll get you up a few more times today."

Getting out of the room and moving administered an enormous mental boost.

———

When Betsy and her mom left after spending most of the evening, the secluded hospital room became my solitary confinement. It was a lonely, desolate feeling I'd never experienced. I'm used to having people around and not having cancer.

Many nights, I'd get up at approximately 2 a.m. and walk through the eerie, remote, antiseptic hallways that appeared filthy from fluorescent hallway lighting, temporarily removing myself from reality and the unwanted solitude in my room.

That night, at 2:07 a.m., I got up and exited my chamber, turned left, and walked toward the C-2 exit. I took a right just before the exit and traversed the long hallway. I saw bright lighting ahead and approached a nurses' station.

"Which way is the twenty-four-hour Starbucks?" I asked the nurse.

"You should go with decaf at this hour," she said.

"Is this a nurses' station or a space station?" The saucer-shaped area looked like the bridge on the Starship Enterprise.

"You're also an alien?"

"I am your friend, Miss Martian with pretty red hair."

"Hello, I'm Haley," she said, smiled, and stretched out her hand.

"Hello Haley, I'm Chris." We shook hands.

"Chris, how are you?"

"It's nice to get out of my lonesome man cave and move."

"I understand. Good for you. I'm glad you're able to walk freely."

"Human interaction is as important as walking, even for us aliens," I mentioned after talking for a few minutes. "I've enjoyed chatting. I'll see you again, Haley."

"Chris, you're so much fun. I look forward to next time."

"Thanks." That short visit was a welcome respite from isolation before I resumed my unaccompanied walk through the cold, inhospitable-looking hospital hallways.

"Mr. Hennessy, you've been cleared to chow down tonight," Beth announced on day three post-surgery.

"Halleluiah."

Betsy brought us organic, lean, restaurant hamburgers with sweet potato fries to feast on. I savored every bite and cleared my plate.

"How was that?" Betsy asked.

"The best grub ever. Thanks so much."

Harrison and Hendrix walked through the open door. "My men. Thanks so much for coming to see the ole dad."

"Oh man, we missed the burgers," Hendrix said.

"Glad you got food, Dad," Harrison followed and elbowed Hendrix in the bicep. "How are you feeling?"

"I'm fine. Let's walk, and you'll see how well I'm doing."

Betsy and my sons walked out of the room. I followed, took one step into the hallway, and stopped.

"Are you okay?" Hendrix asked.

Nausea and exhaustion suddenly overtook me. I began to walk but felt worn out and sluggish. *Two seconds ago, I was fine.*

The usual ten-minute stroll around the wing turned into a twenty-minute circuit of struggle. Plodding was the only speed at which I could move. My sons probably thought I was getting around great for a ninety-year-old.

"Love you," Harrison said, hugging me when we returned to my room.

"Love you, Pops," Hendrix said teary-eyed, and they left.

"You should also leave," I told Betsy and lay down.

She came to my side, took my hand, reached down, and kissed my cheek. "I love you."

My gaze followed her as she walked out the door and closed it. Seconds later, my eyes closed, and I slept until 2 a.m. I had no desire or energy to leave the room. I turned over, rested my head on the pillow, and went back to sleep.

I awoke that morning feeling worse than the previous night. An inviting cup of coffee sat on a tray with a breakfast I wouldn't eat—an unripe piece of fruit, fatty bacon, watery scrambled eggs, and cold toast—hospital cuisine at its foulest.

Missing my coffee ritual and wanting to feel a bit of normalcy, I grabbed the decorative disposable cup and took a gulp. *Where did they get this stuff?* It tasted disgusting, like a throwback blend from the 1700s when coffee was bitter and tart and called syrup of soot.

Despite the repulsive aftertaste, I deserved a cup of coffee and drank the entire beverage.

Betsy arrived at 10 a.m. with her mom. "How's Hannah's daddy this morning?"

I grinned slightly and sat up. Betsy gladly helped me dress for our morning walk. I stood but had to sit back down on the bed. Before long, I had to lie down and could barely move. Acute nausea and a massive headache followed.

Nurse Beth came in. "Mr. Hennessy, please lift your shirt so I can see your belly," she said. After I did, she looked startled and said, "Oh my, it's expanding outward, making it appear as if you were seven months pregnant. I've never seen this."

"What does it mean?" I asked, then lunged my head over and vomited viciously into the colossal silver bowl she'd placed on the side of my bed.

The aftertaste from that dreadful cup of coffee had returned to haunt me. Throwing up and having that putrid aftertaste was icing on the cake of doom.

Unfortunately, they'd given me the okay to eat solid food before my digestive system resumed functioning, and I was being poisoned to death.

"Can you give me anti-nausea medication?" I asked Beth.

"I'm so sorry, Mr. Hennessy, but you've used your limit. The doctors are in emergency surgery and can't be disturbed. There's nothing I can do until we can communicate with them."

I turned to Betsy. "This is worse than food poisoning." I could barely speak. "It feels like I'm slipping away and dying." I vomited again.

For the next two hours, I lay there suffering and continuously moaning while Betsy and Mom sat next to me. Betsy kept her hand on my thigh.

At 12:30 p.m., Betsy said, "Honey, I'm going to grab lunch with Mom."

"No! Please don't go. I need your touch." I looked at Betsy. She looked at me and squeezed my thigh.

"I'll get lunch and bring it back." Betsy's mom smiled and left.

"You've got this, baby," Betsy said. "I'm here for you. Keep persevering. This will end, and you're going to be okay."

I nodded, groaning—feeling woozy with dizziness and weak in absolute agony while sweating profusely with category-ten abdominal pain. My head felt as if a vice were squeezing it, which added to my misery. *I've gotta hold on, I've gotta hold on, I've gotta hold on.*

Mom brought back lunch. Betsy ate with one hand on me and the other negotiating her turkey sandwich.

At 2:35 p.m., Beth said, "I need to see how your stomach is doing," and lifted my shirt. The astonished look on Betsy's and Beth's faces told me the bad news. "It's presenting as if you are eight or nine months pregnant."

At 4:18 p.m., Beth followed Doctor Peterkin into my room. "Mr. Hennessy, I'm so sorry for the long delay. We were involved in two emergency crises," he said, looking at my stomach and cringing. "It appears we've run into another."

I wasn't upset or angry. I'd waited patiently. After persevering through hell, it was now my turn.

"Beth is going to perform gastric suctioning, an emergency procedure to drain the toxic substances from your stomach."

"I'm going to stick this plastic tube into your left nostril," Beth said, "and down your throat, threading it through your esophagus and into your stomach, creating suction and siphoning out the poisonous waste."

I would never let anyone stick anything into my nostrils unless it was a life-or-death situation. Unfortunately, this was a life-or-death situation.

"Are you ready?"

"Go for it," I murmured.

She pushed the tube into my nostril and down my throat, scraping the inside of my nasal passage and sending a sweaty, bloody stream down my face. I continued moaning and throwing up abominable liquid. *I've gotta hold on, I've gotta hold on, I've gotta hold on.* It's what I told myself non-stop, like on auto-replay.

After pushing and prodding for thirty minutes, Beth stood tall and let go of the tube, looking haggard like a soldier on the front line. "I'm so sorry. This is not working," she said, breathing heavily. "I must pull the tube out and try the other nostril."

You're kidding me!

"Is that okay?"

No, I'll lie here and die. "Do it," I whispered.

Beth pulled the tube from my left nostril and went for the right. I dismissed the previous thirty minutes as if it had never happened. *I've gotta hold on, I've gotta hold on, I've gotta hold on.*

A group of nurses and medical staff had gathered in the doorway, like a crowd witnessing the scene of a car accident. I endured thirty-five more minutes of abuse, in and out of consciousness, whimpering when awake. Beth finally maneuvered the tube into my belly. The magnificent sound of suction spilled into my ears, waking me. The crowd clapped and cheered in the background as the poisonous liquid gushed into a large container.

My eyes opened to the stream of liquid waste spilling from the tube into the jug near my bed. I was too spent to move. *I did it! I held on! It's over!*

The nausea gradually subsided, and soon it was gone. Although I was depleted mentally and physically, the feeling of relief was remarkable. *If I can get through that, I can get through anything.*

"You need to rest. It's probably a good time for Mom and me to leave," Betsy said.

I nodded. Sleep was imminent, even with the tube still in place.

17

COURTYARD DATE AND A FAMILY REUNION

When Beth arrived at my bedside the next day, she said, "Hey champ, how are you doing?"

"Much better than yesterday."

"I'm sorry you had to suffer so horribly. You're my hero, Chris Hennessy."

"You did the dirty work. I'd never be able to do that."

"It was teamwork."

"Human synergy."

Beth smiled, and we fist-bumped.

"When can we remove the tube from my nose?" I asked.

"Would right now work?"

"I've never been more ready."

Beth yanked the tube and held it in her hands.

"I'm topless. I mean tubeless."

"Unfortunately, Mr. Tubeless," Beth said, "if you don't muster up a poop by later today, we must reinsert it."

"God, please assist my digestive tract in getting back on track. Let the crap flow freely and effortlessly."

Beth smiled.

Soon, my belly began to churn, and a while later came a delightful excretion.

The following day, I woke up at 7 a.m. and felt energetic. I decided to visit my neighbor Willoughby. I'd passed his room several times, waved at him as he lay in bed, and briefly chatted once. A young man seemed to always be at his bedside.

I knocked on the open door, and two smiling faces greeted me. "Please come in."

"How are my favorite neighbors this morning?" I asked and entered.

"We woke up alive," Willoughby said, raising his arms, chuckling, then taking a breath and holding it before letting it out. "I'm blessed to be in this hospital and to have my son Lucas with me. Thanks for asking."

"I witnessed your entire episode yesterday, Mr. Hennessy," Lucas said. "I'd never seen a person endure such agony. I'm delighted to see you. How are you today?"

"Please call me Chris. Yes, it was torture, but I got through it and am ready for the next challenge."

"What brought you to Stanford Hospital?" Willoughby asked.

"I knew I couldn't get in on grades. By having my cancerous prostate removed, I can say I went to Stanford."

They laughed heartily.

"We're praying they got all of it," I said, "but we won't know until the pathology report populates. May I ask what you're battling?"

"Advanced pancreatic cancer," Willoughby shared. "The tumor is large and spreading, even though it was diagnosed only four months ago. Unfortunately, it's a difficult cancer to diagnose early. At this point, there's not much they can do."

"I'm so sorry." I bowed and prayed, "Father, please give Willoughby and me the attitude and strength to beat cancer. Please help us get out of here to be home with our families."

"I love your vibe, Chris. We can heal for real, and I'm not joking," he said, then coughed for several seconds.

After a few more minutes, I wrapped up our conversation. "Gentlemen, I really enjoyed our chat." I gave a thumbs-up. "I'm going to head back to my room. My wife will be here soon."

"You're always welcome, and we'll leave the light on," Willoughby said, and we all laughed.

Beth was still in my room when Betsy arrived at 10 a.m. Betsy didn't notice or mention my tubeless face, and I didn't bring it up.

"Don't get comfortable," I announced. "We're going on our walk that never happened yesterday."

"I wish we could go outside," Betsy said. "It's sunny and in the low 70s."

"You two need to make your way to the courtyard." Beth made a good case as to why. "There's a walkway through gardens and benches. It'll be a relaxing and romantic date."

"Let's do it," I said. The outdoors was much needed, away from recirculated air and fluorescent lighting. "Thanks for the tip." I stood slowly, felt queasy, and realized my right foot ached. I didn't twist or hurt it; the pain materialized out of nowhere. Despite that, I was excited about leaving the room and ignored the discomfort. "We'll see you later, Beth."

We sauntered out of my room, up the hallway, out of the C-2 unit, and into the hospital. The last time I passed through those doors was post-surgery, still unconscious from the anesthesia. I enjoyed the plethora of passersby, some in scrub suits and others in civilian clothing.

We came to the indoor quad where mellow, live grand piano music bounced off the high ceilings with fabulous acoustics and feel-good energy.

"There's the courtyard," I said and pointed downstairs. We then headed to outdoor freedom.

Majestic buildings designed in the mission revival style encircled the unroofed courtyard. Their earth-tone stucco surfaces added a textured wall finish that mimicked California's Spanish missions built in the late 1700s and early 1800s. Meticulously landscaped grounds surrounded four empty benches.

We walked the short path around the courtyard, enjoying

gorgeous vistas, and then sat facing brilliant western redbud and jacaranda trees. Their vibrant shades of blue and purple created a delightful contrast to the structures in the background and the blue skies above.

The refreshing breeze, splendid temperature, and being alone with Betsy in a tranquil and peaceful atmosphere were what I coveted. We cuddled in natural noiselessness. I closed my eyes, and the sun's invisible beams of infinite energy rolled over me for the first time in days, transmitting a welcomed dose of warmth and comfort. We sat there for an hour, sharing fresh air and abundant natural sunlight. Barely moving and only occasionally speaking, we both cherished those moments on the first of our treasured courtyard dates. The pleasant white noise of the occasional train, small plane, and Harley Davidson in the distant background tranquilized us.

"How's Hannah?" I asked.

"She feels great," Betsy said, patting her tummy. "She wants her daddy to come home."

I touched Betsy's belly and said, "Hey baby, I love you. We can't wait to see you. Your daddy and mommy will give you infinite love and kisses."

I was thankful to be alive. "Life as usual, right, honey? I love you."

"I love you, too."

I had earned this time and didn't want it to end. However, Betsy and I had an inside date with the shower. My grimy self hadn't showered in several days.

"I don't care to leave, but it's time to head back," I said, detaching myself from Betsy.

"The shower awaits. I'm ready to help wash my man."

We stood and hugged. "This was the best hour," I said, looking around. "We're going to make this a daily ritual." I took Betsy's hand. We walked through the path, back inside, and returned to my room.

"Remove your gown and underwear," Betsy said as we walked through the door and into my room. "I'll grab the washcloth, towels, and dry clothing."

Betsy went into the bathroom and turned the water on. I entered and felt the warm, moist air, then immersed myself in the deluge of drenching hot water.

"Let's get your naked butt onto a bench," Betsy said before climbing into the shower and beginning to scrub my belly area close to the wound.

I looked down by mistake and saw the scar. "It looks like a war wound from below my belly button to the bottom of my lower belly."

"I'm sorry. It's not a pleasant sight. Let's both try to avoid glancing at it."

The gushing hot water invigorated me, like diving into the medicinal ocean after a long sunbathing session.

Betsy washed my shoulders, back, arms, legs, feet, and hands, and scratched, massaged, and scrubbed my head. There's no way I could have done it myself. Her touch was restorative, like a professional massage therapist at a ritzy spa. After being scrub-a-dub-dubbed, I exited the shower feeling clean and revitalized.

That fabulous day after a horrible day continued into the evening. Harrison and Hendrix brought Hadley. My little pumpkin had estranged herself from us two years earlier without reason or explanation. I couldn't care less about the past, welcomed her, and thanked God for bringing her to me.

We chatted and laughed while reminiscing about favorite memories, friends, and relatives.

There's nothing I loved more than Betsy and my kids. Right then, they were all with me.

18

ATTITUDE IS EVERYTHING

After a day of fantastic activity, I was worn out and ready to sleep. As soon as my family left, I nodded off.

I awoke at 2 a.m., my usual time, got out of bed, and exited my room. As I approached the end of C-2, I decided to stay the course and venture out again.

Like leaving the house on a Saturday morning on my bike without my parents knowing or caring where I'd be most of the day, I had a fabulous feeling of freedom.

Wandering aimlessly throughout the hospital reminded me of running an unfamiliar cross-country course. I enjoyed the trails and having yet to learn where the next turn led.

What a treat to have the entire hospital to myself. Nobody played the lonely piano in the vast, empty atrium. The elevators were still, and no aroma drifted from the cafeteria. I enjoyed being alone in the eerie ambiance.

I headed back to C-2. As I passed Willoughby's room, I saw Lucas sleeping on a chair before his dad's bed. His head lay awkwardly on the arm of the chair. The rest of him was in the fetal position, except his dangling feet.

A nurse outside my room worked at her medical workstation on wheels. I read her name badge before greeting her. "Menee, I'm Chris Hennessy, and this is my dwelling," I said and pointed. "I'm glad you're loitering here."

"Excuse me, Mr. Hennessy," she said, moving away from my door.

"I believe you misunderstood. The nurse vibe in the hallway makes me feel less lonely. Please feel free to work here and block my door anytime."

"I understand." Menee smiled. "Thank you. How are you feeling? I heard about yesterday's incident."

"I'm fine. It was a team effort. Together, we emptied the poison from my stomach."

"Everyone was very concerned. I'm so glad for a victorious outcome."

"Thanks, Menee."

She must have noticed a look of concern on my face. "How can I help you?"

"Willoughby's son Lucas has been sleeping on a small chair. He's there right now," I said as I led her to Willoughby's room.

She peered into the room. "That's terrible sleeping posture."

"Can we get him a blanket and a couple of pillows?" I asked.

"I'll take care of it. Thanks for a kind gesture."

"I'm happy to help. Lucas is dedicated to his dad and deserves some comfort. I'll see you again."

"Have a good night, Mr. Hennessy."

I wanted more social interaction and headed to the nurses' station to see if Haley was there. After walking away from Menee, I took a right near the C-2 exit, spotted the brilliant light at the end of the hall, and walked toward it. "Is this the Starbucks drive-through?" I asked, approaching the counter.

"Mr. Hennessy." Haley lifted her head and smiled. "I'm so happy you're okay. I was worried about you."

"You were there?"

"No, I heard about it. The tube shoved in your nose didn't sound like fun."

"It was the most difficult challenge of my life. I'm proud of persevering. That mondo feat fulfills my soul. I'll always remember and know I can defeat other difficulties. Thanks for caring."

"Your attitude brings me much joy."

"You know what would bring me joy?"

"What's that?"

"One hot dark roast coffee with half-and-half and a fresh bagel. Can you help a patient?"

"I could bring you our contaminated coffee blend," her bubbly voice said and chuckled.

"Someone certainly doesn't care about the patients' coffee. I drank a cup yesterday morning. When I became ill, the aftertaste added to the agony."

"That's horrible. Our coffee needs a doctor."

"Or a mortician."

"Yes," she said and giggled.

"Before driving away from this drive-through," I slyly looked to the left and hesitated, "I must tell you," I said, then looked to the right and back to Haley, "our conversation worked better than coffee." I winked at her.

"That's what I like hearing." We slapped five. "Your mindset is off the charts. I'm proud to know you."

"Thanks for listening. C-2 rocks. I'll see you soon."

"Take care of yourself."

I departed and felt like jumping and clicking my feet, but I dawdled happily ahead with a gunshot-like wound in my gut. When I was back in isolation, I removed my Nike Air Max, put on a clean undershirt, lay down, and sleep came effortlessly.

"Are you having fun?" I said after being aroused by Beth servicing my IV line.

"Good morning."

"Good morning." I yawned, lifted my arms, and stretched. "May I ask the time?"

She looked at her phone. "It's 6:20 a.m. Michael Jackson's death was caused by a lethal combination of sedatives and propofol. The Giants won last night, and the weather will be as gorgeous today as yesterday."

"Thanks for the news, sports, and weather reports. That's so sad about Michael Jackson," I said, shaking my head.

"You're very welcome. I'm a huge MJ fan, and that news hit hard," she said dejectedly.

Before I could respond, she asked, "Did the courtyard date happen?"

"Yes. It was wonderful. Thanks, Beth."

"Tell me about it."

"The ambiance of the quad in windless sunshine, outside by ourselves, was essential. It was a date I'll always remember. Thanks for the recommendation."

"I knew you'd enjoy it." She smiled and clapped. "It's surprising how few patients take advantage of the courtyard."

"They're missing out. It was quite beneficial. After an hour outdoors, Betsy helped me manage a much-needed, heavenly shower."

"You're blessed to have her. I see so many patients without such love and support."

"I agree. Without her, there would have been no courtyard or shower dates. I'll escort Queen Betsy on our second courtyard date this afternoon."

"Following your worst day with extraordinary days. Way to go, Hennessys!"

"Beth, last night, I asked Menee to bring Willoughby's son a blanket and pillows." I looked into her eyes, concerned. "He's been sleeping on a small chair. Have you seen them this morning?"

"I haven't. Let's see if Menee pulled through." I got out of bed and followed Beth to the entrance of Willoughby's room. Lucas was sleeping comfortably on a cot with pillows and blankets.

"Way to go, Menee. This makes me happy," I said, and we returned to my room.

"Haley!" I cried out when she came through my open door holding three cups of fresh, hot Starbucks coffee. "This is a neat surprise."

"I finished my shift and went to Starbucks," she said, handing each of us a beverage. I sat on my bed, and my nurse buddies were on chairs beside me. "Let's enjoy our coffee and chat for a few minutes."

"I'll drink to that." I raised my grande drip with two tablespoons of half-and-half. "A toast to our dark roasts and us." Our cups clinked, and we took celebratory sips.

"How well do you guys know my Pee Pee?" I asked.

"Excuse me?" Beth asked. They looked at each other and cracked up.

"Doctor Pee Pee," I said, and they belly laughed.

Beth took a swig of coffee. "He listens and cares about the staff and our patients."

"He even consumes the patient's food and our coffee," I said.

Beth spit out the liquid in her mouth, and Haley choked on the beverage and saliva that went down the wrong pipe while laughing.

"We patients love him." I gave a thumbs-up, and so did they.

"Chris, you have a gift that we rarely see in patients," Haley said. "Laughter and positivity." She and Beth nodded.

"Attitude is everything." I held up my cup and gulped down the delicious, caffeinated beverage.

"What was the best thing about your courtyard date? Beth told me you two were going out there."

"Being in crisp outdoor air in sunlight with my wife."

Beth and Haley looked at each other and smiled empathetically.

"I'm glad this worked out," Haley said, guzzling the remaining contents of her cup. "I need sleep."

"Thanks for the coffee and conversation, Hay," I said.

We stood and group-hugged.

"You two have a great day." Haley waved as she walked out the door and headed home.

"I need to take your vitals before continuing my rounds," Beth said.

"Please don't take my vitals."

"Why?"

"I need them."

19

GOING HOME CANCER-FREE!

I'd just put on my shoes when Doctor Peterkin arrived. He wore jeans and a T-shirt. "Good morning, Mr. Hennessy."

"Doctor Peterkin, isn't Sunday your day off? I wasn't expecting to see you today."

"Yes, but I wanted to give you an update. How are you?"

"I'm good. Betsy's on the way. We'll hike to the courtyard for my required fresh air and sunshine. This radical prostatectomy journey has taught me to never take the outdoors for granted."

"That sounds like fun and certainly is medicinal." He paused. "And it's likely your last outing. I've arranged for you to be discharged tomorrow morning," he said, nodding and smiling.

A surge of exhilaration rushed over me.

Before I could say anything, he said, "Mr. Hennessy, there's another news flash. Your pathology report is clear. Your prostate was one ball of cancer. However, none of it escaped. We got it all." He pumped his fist like he'd sunk a putt to win the Masters Golf Championship.

I'm going home without cancer. The relief that washed over me was indescribable. "That's the most amazing newsflash I've ever heard."

My face turned serious. "I'm so glad we chose Stanford. Mission accomplished." We fist-bumped.

"This couldn't be a better report. I'm very happy for you. I'll see you in my office two weeks from tomorrow for our first follow-up."

"Doctor Peterkin, thanks so much for everything. You and your team are the best."

"Mr. Hennessy, thanks for being an exemplary patient. Your antics and enthusiasm uplifted C-2 staff and patients." We shook hands, then he turned around and enjoyed his day off. He was obviously and deservedly feeling good about himself.

I stood, took a step away from my bed, and cringed in pain after stepping off my right foot. I sat back down, removed my right shoe, pulled down the sock, and peered at my swollen, black-and-purple-colored ankle. I'd done my research and knew there was a 2 percent chance of this being a DVT blood clot. *There's no other explanation.* I kept this development to myself at the time. I just wanted to go home.

Betsy strolled in with a smile and halo around her beautiful head. I quickly put on my right sock, lowered my head, and acted out a fake distressed look. "I've got some news," I said, lifted my head, and looked into my angel's eyes. "Doctor Peterkin dropped by this morning." I paused and smiled. "We're going home tomorrow!"

Betsy broke into tears. "I wish this was tomorrow morning."

We hugged like we did four months ago when the pregnancy test was positive.

"There's more. The pathology report was clear. They got all the cancer."

Betsy looked upward. "God, you're amazing. You've answered our prayers." We both cried.

"Daddy's coming home, Hannah," I said, teary-eyed and stroking Betsy's belly. "I'll brush my teeth, and then we'll continue our celebration in the courtyard." I put on my right shoe, went into the bathroom, and brushed my teeth, filled with anticipation for the new chapter of my life that awaited me at home.

"My dear Betsy, may I escort you for one last excursion to the courtyard?" I asked, walking out of the bathroom and bowing.

"Of course," she said, taking my right arm with her left. "It's an honor to accompany my cancer-free husband to the quad."

I stepped forward and winced. My right foot ached fiercely, but Betsy didn't notice. Once I was in motion, it felt better.

"The pleasure is mine," I said, and arm in arm we sauntered through the busy hallways, into the foyer downstairs, and stepped out the door. I stopped, breathed in as much outside air as my lungs would accept, and let it out slowly. "Mrs. Hennessy, let's traverse the trail opposite our usual direction."

"Changing things up. I like it, Mr. Hennessy."

We walked the loop around the courtyard, approached our bench, and sat in delicious sunlight. Betsy took out her pocketknife and carved our initials on the back of the bench—CH, BH, and HH, 08/09.

"I didn't know you could do that," I said and snapped a selfie of Betsy, me, and her work.

"Neither did I."

"We must come back here and show Hannah," I said, showing Betsy the photo on my phone."

"Aw, I love it, and Hannah will too. We'll definitely come back with her."

"How's your mom and dad?"

"They send their love. Dad can't wait to play golf with you. Mom said she'll bake your favorite lemon meringue pie this weekend, and Dad will grill turkey burgers with homemade sweet potato fries."

"Oh, baby. Home cooking is why I can't wait to get out of here." We chuckled.

"Hey, let's head inside for your shower," Betsy said.

"You read my mind. That'll help me sleep well and be ready to go home."

"Yes, I want a clean man in our house."

"Let's do it."

I was up early and ecstatic while preparing to take one last walk as a Stanford Hospital patient. Ignoring my painful foot, I took off, feeling confident and energetic. I was excited to see Haley approaching. "Haley, good morning. Where are you off to?"

"Good morning," she said, looking exhausted. "I'm heading to mi casa."

"I'm so glad to see you. I'm also headed home in a couple of hours."

"Awesome, Chris." She smiled enthusiastically. "You can finally go to a real Starbucks."

"Yes. I can't wait to see my coffeehouse buddies. I've got some great stories to tell."

"Make sure to tell them how great the nurses were."

"The nurses in C-2 deserve medals of honor. The doctors rip us patients apart, and the nurses get us back on our feet. I will always have much love and respect for nurses."

"That warms my heart. I'll miss your midnight-hours pass-by. You always brightened my night."

"Our late-night chats were crucial and calming. Thanks for putting up with me." We laughed and hugged.

Haley left, and I headed to Willoughby's room. The last time I saw him or his son was when we chatted the other day. I knocked on the closed door, which was usually open. No answer. I opened the door, and the room was empty.

I returned to the nurse's station. "Ma'am, I knocked on Willoughby's door to say goodbye, and there was no answer. I opened the door and found the room vacant."

"Oh, Mr. Hennessy," she said with a terrified look, "Willoughby passed away yesterday. I'm so sorry. His son packed up and left last night."

"Oh, I see. Thanks." My heart hurt for a fallen fellow cancer battler. "How was his son Lucas?"

"I don't know. Willoughby was sleeping, and they came in for vitals, and he was gone. I'm not sure if his son was there at the time."

I walked away very slowly, with my head down, to my room. *I'm so sorry for Willoughby and Lucas.*

Betsy arrived at noon and helped me pack. Only seconds later, Beth walked in with an unhappy face. "We're going to miss you." She hugged me and looked at Betsy. "You two go have a fabulous life together."

"Thanks, Beth," I said, too choked up to muster another word.

"Beth, you're a saint," Betsy said. "Thanks for lifting and helping Chris. He'll never forget you, and neither will I."

Beth and Betsy looked at each other. "Thank you, Betsy." Beth looked at me. "Stay your upbeat, hilarious self." Then Beth started crying, as did Betsy. It's fascinating how different feelings and memories can make us laugh or cry. Thank God we're creatures that can show and feel emotions.

I looked back at my bed and thought of when Beth thrust the plastic tube into my nostrils. The reflection quickly dissipated. I smiled at Beth, and her teary-eyed face smiled back.

Betsy and I walked out of C-2 and Stanford Hospital, and Betsy drove us home.

We entered the house, put our stuff on the couch in the living room, and headed to the bedroom. I was optimistic but weak and worn out mentally and physically. I knew there'd be more pain, suffering, and troubled times ahead. But I was home and cancer-free. Screw the future. I chose to live only in that moment.

We lay down, took a wonderful nap in our bed, and then resumed life as usual.

20

DEFYING DOCTOR'S ORDERS

Betsy entered the bedroom at 8 a.m. "Are you leaving for work?" I asked.

"Yes. How'd you sleep?"

"Excellent. I missed our bed."

"Your bed and your wife really missed you." She kissed me gently on the forehead. "Have a great day. I'm so happy you're home. I love you."

"Love you, too." As soon as I heard Betsy's car leave, I got out of bed. I felt fabulous and ready to embrace the normalcy of my life once again.

The doctor ordered me not to leave the house or drive for ten days until they removed the catheter. I ignored the instructions to be out of the house and around people.

I removed the catheter bag from my belt, pushed the plastic tube down the inside of my pants and out of the bottom, and hooked up the portable catheter bag inside the hem. That way, I could visit my beloved Starbucks without the catheter being noticed, and Betsy wouldn't even know I had left the house.

I grabbed my wallet, left the nest, got in my car, placed the key into the ignition, turned it quickly to the right, and had go-power.

Leaving when I wasn't supposed to thrilled me, like when I was an unlicensed teenager and snuck out of the house to take the family station wagon for a joy ride. I gently pressed my foot on the gas pedal and remained wary of my leg while driving to Starbucks.

I parked, exited my car, adjusted the catheter, and walked through the parking area and into Starbucks. I saw several of my coffeehouse buddies sitting at our unofficial table. They rushed out of their chairs and greeted me with handshakes and hugs, making the trip worth it.

"Hey guys, please sit back down and let me grab my first cup of real coffee in almost two weeks." I got in line and noticed my portable catheter bag lying on the floor. I reached down, picked it up, and hooked it back into place.

"Sit down, Henn, your coffee is on me," Big Joe said, his words a comforting reminder of the support I had from my friends.

"Thanks so much, big man. Hurry up, I can't wait to chat."

I sat down at our table with five others. Joe delivered my grande dark drip. "Here you go, Henn. They didn't have coffee in the hospital?"

"The hospital coffee was worse than the food," I said with a sour face, and they laughed. I noticed an odd moisture sensation on my left foot. I'd forgotten about the catheter. When I looked down, the catheter bag was on the ground again. This time, it had opened, and fluid seeped onto the floor, twisting and turning around the folks in line who were trying to avoid my puddle of pee.

I stood, reached down, and noticed several folks looking at me. I picked up the bag. "Spilled my lemonade," I said, smiling. Then I waved at them and hooked the bag back onto my pants. I wasn't embarrassed. After enduring cancer surgery and the entire ordeal in the hospital, my mind rarely ever again experienced embarrassment.

Every head turned but one.

"Chris, how are you?" It was the familiar voice of Betsy's co-worker and best friend, Rachel.

Busted. "Oh, Rachel, I'm alive and well, and you're not at work."

"I had a doctor's appointment. I'm headed in now. Are you okay? I see you've had a little accident."

Ugh. "I'm fine. Everything's cool."

"Take care," she said as she walked to the barista to place her order. "I'll say hello to Betsy."

Yes, you will. "Love to Mark," I said, giving my best fake smile. "We'll have to get together soon." I returned to the table.

When Betsy gets home, she'll pain-in-the-neck me. I could see it play out in my mind. "Why did you leave the house? You had specific instructions to stay home."

If I don't react harshly, she'll listen and understand that I need the freedom of not being confined to the house.

The staff cleaned my mess. "Thank you so much," I said and smiled.

I sat again, and all six friends asked questions simultaneously. "Okay, guys, one at a time."

"How are you feeling?" Paul asked.

"How am I feeling?" I repeated. "Ecstatic. Like I returned home from war. Alive. Without PTSD. I'm so glad it's over and I'm out of there. I'm not supposed to leave the house until after they remove the catheter, but I needed to see you guys and socialize." Their eyes were laser-focused, and they listened intently. "So, bring out the chips and cards. Deal them out, Big Joe."

"Ha! That's what I'm talking about."

"Did they get it all?" Will asked.

"You're looking at a cancer-free coffee buddy," I announced, the relief evident in my voice.

"Yeah!" They roared like two dozen men in a sports bar cheering for a touchdown.

I changed the subject to sports, and we spent the rest of our hour discussing the status of the San Francisco 49ers and Giants.

"Gentlemen, I'm going to head back home to the office. I've got plenty of work to catch up on."

"We all need to get on with our day," Big Joe said. "We're so glad to have you back, Henn."

"You guys have me feeling fantastic. See you tomorrow."

I drove home and looked forward to getting back into my office.

After parking in the garage, I went through the back door and into the kitchen, opened the refrigerator, grabbed my bottomless bottle of water, opened my office door, put the bottle down, and pressed the on-button to my desktop computer. My plan was to return to work mode gradually. I attended to emails and client needs and made a few phone calls. *I'll get back to editing and marketing tomorrow.*

At 5:30 p.m., I saw Betsy pull into the driveway from my office window. I went to the door and greeted my baby.

"How was your work session?" Betsy asked and walked into the house, smiling.

"It was nice to get back into action. I'm pretty caught up and feel good about where I am."

"I'm proud of you. Let me warm up the leftovers, and we'll sit down to dinner."

I returned to my office, took a few minutes to wrap up, put my computer to sleep, and headed to the dinner table.

"I heard you were at Starbucks this morning," Betsy said after serving last night's spaghetti and meatballs.

Here comes the interrogation.

"How'd that go?"

"Besides the minor spill, which I'm sure Rachel told you about, it was the best morning I've had since pre-surgery."

"Yes, Chris, but I was worried to death after speaking with Rachel."

"It was a spur-of-the-moment decision, but it was necessary. I felt so happy getting out of here and socializing a bit. Moving forward, for my mental health, I need to be out of here for an hour or two in the morning. Physically, the worst that can happen is a leak."

"Okay, but please be very careful."

"Yes, dear." *Phew.*

21

THE MOST PAINFUL SECOND AND RECOVERY SETBACKS

Two weeks after my release date, I drove to Stanford Hospital for my first post-surgery blood work and catheter removal. The PSA blood test reading was .03. We had hoped for a zero, indicating no cancer cells, but a reading of .03 is still considered good. If subsequent tests showed a rise in PSA levels, it would indicate the cancer was still present.

They sent me to an exam room to remove the catheter. I was eager to be free from that hindrance.

"Mr. Hennessy, please remove your pants and underwear," the nurse said after she arrived.

"I can see this will be an exciting first date."

"Yes, I'm a professional first dater." She checked my surgical wound. "Hmm, it's slightly infected," she said. "That's normal. Just keep it covered."

"Is this going to take long? Will it hurt?" She looked into my eyes, and just as I thought she was going to answer my question, she grabbed the plastic tube without my noticing and yanked the catheter out in one split second.

"Ow!" I screamed. I wouldn't be surprised if the students across the street at Stanford University heard my piercing outburst. It was easily the most painful second of my life. "That was brilliant. I'm glad you got it over with without warning."

"It works every time. Have a great day, Mr. Hennessy."

Despite the doctor's caution to avoid the elliptical for six weeks, I was determined to resume normal activities. The surgery area didn't hinder walking, and with the catheter gone, I was ready to take the first steps toward recovery.

The morning after the quick-handed nurse yanked my catheter, I drove five minutes and arrived in the parking area where the bridge crossed Los Alamitos Creek, the spot on our trail where I proposed to Betsy. I turned left into the gravel parking area, parked, and walked up the stairs. *There's me on my knees and jubilant, blubbering Betsy.*

I set my watch's timer to one minute, pressed the start button, lifted my right leg, placed my foot onto the wooden post, bent down, and gently stretched a rigid hamstring. The simple act relieved my pent-up muscle tension and brought pleasure from the discomfort. Once the alarm sounded, I repeated the stretch on my left hamstring. My legs and lower back were more flexible and ready to go.

Being outside and releasing my suppressed energy worked wonders for me. I held back and walked only one slow mile on Tuesday, Wednesday, and Thursday. I rested on Friday and walked a faster two miles on Saturday and Sunday. Astonishingly, the walking helped boost my mood and energy. Mentally and physically, everything felt great except for my ailing foot. I wasn't yet ready to accept reality and kept trucking in denial.

Betsy and I drove to Almaden Lake late Monday morning of the following week. We parked, grabbed each other's hands, and steered ourselves to the stretching area.

"Lake or bridge?" I asked. Her answer determined where we'd start our trail trek.

"Lake. It's a one-mile loop."

"Let's do it. We'll go around twice."

"I'm worried about you," Betsy said while we stretched.

"Why?" I still hadn't told her about my foot issue.

"Are you okay to film the wedding on Saturday?"

For the first time in more than one thousand gigs, I had to cancel my services for the wedding the previous weekend.

"Harrison and Hendrix are excited to assist me and make some money. I can't wait to get back. They'll do the lifting, and I'll stay focused and aware. I'm up to it and ready—very ready."

"That sounds fine. I trust you, but please be careful."

I hugged her and asked, "Hannah's due date is still December 7?"

"Yes."

"It seems such a long way off."

"It gives us plenty of time to prepare her room and buy clothes." For the remainder of our walk, we talked non-stop about our parenting plans for Hannah.

I skipped exercising on Wednesday and walked three miles on Thursday. Experiencing a bit of a runner's high, with its ensuing elation, helped my recovery.

Before showering, I looked at my swollen, dark purple foot, and reality struck. It was time to deal with the fact that my foot was not improving. *This is a DVT blood clot. It's time to see Doctor Peterkin.*

"I've got something I need to share," I said to Betsy that night after dinner. I pulled off my sock, revealing my foot.

She gasped. "That's horrific, like your surgery wound." She shook her head. "How long has this been going on?"

"I noticed it in the hospital a few days after surgery."

"Why haven't you said anything?"

"I needed to exercise. I thought it might get better."

"You need to call Stanford tomorrow morning and schedule an appointment to see Doctor Peterkin. Please contact your client and arrange for one of your videography friends to film Saturday's wedding."

"I understand and will do it." Every man should have a strong-willed woman like Betsy for support and guidance.

Keeping my promise, I called Doctor Peterkin's office on Friday morning and scheduled an appointment for Tuesday, September 1, at 10:30 a.m.

I didn't let myself get down or worry excessively about being unable to power walk that weekend. Betsy and I had a fabulous shopping excursion for Hannah and then enjoyed dinner at a favorite local restaurant. Excellent service and fruitful conversation supplemented our fantastic meal.

Although I drove to Stanford on Tuesday, my appointment with Doctor Peterkin didn't happen. Because of Hannah's unexpected birth that day—more than three months premature—I rescheduled for Friday, September 4.

22

MICRO-PREEMIES ARE NICU WARRIORS

Tuesday, September 1, 2009 (Continued from Chapter 1)

After Hannah's birth, the nurses took Betsy to her room, and she fell quickly asleep. I went downstairs for my inaugural visit with my baby girl.

Doctor Powers told me that Hannah was fighting for her life. Thank God they were able to remove the ventilator, her first of several summits to scale. Now, they needed to get her digestive system moving. It seemed like an insurmountable mission.

Doctor Powers also told me that Mommy and Daddy's touch, voice, and scent were more crucial than medical technology.

I arrived at Hannah's side; we could only touch her by sticking an arm through a small hole into the incubator. When my hand reached in and softly stroked her hand, she grasped my index finger and held on, and we connected—three months ahead of schedule. It was a magical feeling of love and attachment that profoundly impacted my life.

After seeing her, I exited the NICU and walked to the elevator to return to Betsy's room. I pressed the up button, and when the elevator doors opened, Betsy's mom and best friend, Rachel, stood there. We hugged. "I'm headed to Betsy's room," I said. "She's fine. I was visiting Hannah."

"Hannah?" Mom asked in disbelief.

"Yes, Mom. Hannah was born about an hour ago. She looks beautiful and is stable."

Neither of them knew Hannah had been born. After what must have been a horrifying two-hour drive from Davis, it took Mom a few minutes to process that her granddaughter had arrived.

Betsy's brother Steve flew in from San Diego, and brothers Joe and Tim had driven from Davis and picked up Steve at San José International Airport. The six of us entered Betsy's room simultaneously. I needed to move a bit and had yet to eat since breakfast. While the family gave love and greetings to Betsy, I excused myself, walked swiftly to my car, and grabbed a power bar and bottle of water. I stood, devoured the bar in four bites, chugged twenty ounces of water, and then speed-walked back to reality.

I entered Betsy's room and peered at the solemn group of folks. When Betsy saw me, she started crying. "Oh, God, even if Hannah makes it out of the hospital, she's going to have cerebral palsy and a lifetime of illness." The room remained silent with all heads down.

I need to uplift us now. I stood and looked at the disheartened faces before me, sipped water, breathed slowly, and presented my second inspirational speech of the day, again unrehearsed.

"Let's not focus on something that hasn't and may not happen. We need to be positive and keep talking to God. Our attitude will help Hannah and inspire her medical team. We'll get through this with a healthy Hannah. God is telling me she'll be fine. We must have faith and believe."

As I finished speaking, there was a noticeable shift in the atmosphere; the collective mood had significantly lifted.

Mom stood. "Betsy, what can I get for you?" she asked.

"Dinner is on me," Steve insisted. "Joe, Tim, and I will bring back a fine meal for everyone."

"That's great. Thanks so much," I said.

Downtown Palo Alto, about a mile away, had many fine restaurants. Betsy's brothers left and returned a short while later with delicious turkey sandwiches on fresh sourdough rolls and a huge salad bowl featuring local romaine lettuce and roasted vegetables. We had a wonderful meal and evening together while enjoying each other's company.

After everyone left, I tucked Betsy in and headed home to do some work.

I remained in an unflappable zone of fortitude and focus, stayed myself, and was passionate about my work and workouts. My attitude helped keep everyone loose and laughing, including the doctors and nurses.

September 2

My Mitsubishi Endeavor maneuvered through rows of visitors' cars in the hospital parking lot. As I drove, I daydreamed about being at the beach with Hannah and Betsy. It was a gorgeous sunny day, and I held Hannah and showed her the giant sandbox. She smiled and wanted to play with the plastic pail and shovel until she noticed the gigantic bathtub. Her delightful, fascinated face lit up as she pointed to the water with her tiny finger.

Because my brain was in imagination mode, I passed an available spot.

I hit the brakes and shifted to reverse like an Indy driver, backed up, stopped, thrust the manual gear shift to drive, veered left, and pulled into my spot. Suddenly, I felt an urge to be with Betsy and Hannah immediately. I got out of the car and speed walked to the entrance, then to the elevator, up to the third floor, and stopped at the NICU's entrance.

The NICU was protected by significantly stupid security measures. I had experienced it the day before.

When I pressed the button, the voice asked, "May I have yours and your baby's name?"

"Chris Hennessy here to see Hannah Hennessy."

The door opened automatically, and I wandered ten yards through a dimly lit, narrow hallway to another door. There were no instructions on how to proceed. *Do they want me to place my driver's license over this scanner?* I put my ID over the scanner, and nothing happened. I scratched my head and looked around to see if I could find any indications or prompts. Nothing. I placed my license's front, back, and all angles on the scanner.

I need to get to Hannah! I turned around and started walking, and then the doors opened quickly. I swung around and ran through, walked the short hallway, took a right when it ended, and finally arrived at the front desk.

"Hello," I said to the expressionless NICU receptionist.

"Mr. Hennessy, may I see your license, NICU ID, and date of birth?"

"February 24, 1957," I said while handing her my ID. She peered at my license and carefully studied it to find any small reason to turn me away. She handed it back without making eye contact.

"Thank you," she said, and the doors opened.

This evening was a similar escapade, except the second time things were familiar, and it was a bit easier. I entered room A. A long row of a dozen incubators lined each side of the room, which was home to babies in the most critical condition, fighting for their lives. Hannah would remain there for several weeks.

Hannah's incubator, the second on the right, featured a hand-written sign with large purple letters that read, "HANNAH," which drew our attention like a highway billboard.

"Hey, sweetheart," I said to Betsy, who was already sitting at Hannah's side. "Are you excited to come home tomorrow?"

"I'm so ready." We hugged, and I sat on the opposite side of the incubator. The panicked feeling of getting there dissipated.

Doctor Powers sauntered over. "Hello, Mr. and Mrs. Hennessy. Hannah is resting comfortably."

"Yes, she is, Doctor Powers," I said. It was good to see his upbeat, confident self.

"Let me share some thoughts."

"Please do."

"I tell this to every parent. Don't be heroes. Stay well rested and keep working. Our staff will take excellent care of Hannah when you two are absent. Hannah needs her parents to be rested and strong. But she certainly needs your presence."

Betsy and I listened and understood.

"Can you explain the tube on her face?" Betsy asked.

"The nasal feeding tube in her right nostril goes down the esophagus and into her tummy," he said, pointing at Hannah's nose. "These tubes are used for babies who are ready to digest breast milk or formula but are not yet able to suck and swallow."

"So, the tube is not currently in use," Betsy said.

"Correct. Hannah is only being fed parenteral nutrition (TPN) via an IV because her digestive system has not begun to function. This morning, we placed 5 ccs (one teaspoon) of Betsy's breast milk into the tube. It was spit up as residual reflux, meaning it wasn't digested. Every drop of Mom's milk would be liquid gold for Hannah. Things will get rolling when she's able to absorb maternal milk."

"Why is the mask covering her face?" Betsy asked, pointing at the CPAP.

"While she doesn't need artificial respiration, she still must have her face covered for the next couple of months with the CPAP. The mask provides respiratory support to treat preterm infants who have underdeveloped lungs. It gently pushes air into her lungs, making it easier for her to breathe."

Hannah looked like an alien. In addition to the CPAP, she wore goggles because the bili light, which shined a dark blue fluorescent light on her face to treat jaundice, was located at the top of her incubator. The goggles and CPAP made it impossible to glimpse more than a trace of her face.

Multiple wires coming from her remained connected to a computer and monitor. The big bandages around her tiny limbs appeared to hold her together. I didn't see any of those impediments; I saw only Hannah, who was gorgeous.

"Thank you so much, Doctor Powers," Betsy said.

We shook hands, and Doctor Powers went back to his office.

Betsy prayed, "God, thank you for teaching us how much we love and need Hannah. Thank you for her strong lungs. We hope for functioning digestion, continued progress, and a healthy Hannah that we can love and care for at home."

"Betsy, you look done for the day," I said at 8:30 p.m. "It's time to go back to your room and rest."

"Good idea. Thanks, honey." She hugged me and said, "Goodnight, Hannah. I love you" before leaving to spend her last night away from home.

Knowing Betsy, she probably passed out seconds after her head touched the pillow. I stayed with Hannah until 12:15 a.m.—long after the other parents had left the NICU. Two nurses on the other side of the room worked quietly among a few dozen babies in incubators, including Hannah.

The extraterrestrial-sounding computer noises enhanced the tranquil ambiance while Hannah held my finger. Eerie and unforgettable high, low, medium, and not-in-any-order inconsistent beeps created a techno-like musical that echoed throughout the NICU, adding a mystical, haunting, somewhat soothing nighttime aura to our sleepy NICU neighborhood.

It reminded me of the sultry nighttime sounds of insects crooning at our summer home in Sound Beach, Long Island, New York. When Mom said, "Lights out" at bedtime, we were left in total darkness. There were no streetlights on the north shore of Long Island in the 1960s and '70s. It was the perfect setting to listen to the performance provided by crickets and katydids right outside our windows. They usually wrapped up around 3 a.m., but we'd been soothed to sleep hours earlier.

The incubator's computer alarm startled me and indicated a possible emergency. When she arrived at the rescue, the nurse looked at me and said, "Mr. Hennessy, please don't fret. It's usually a false alarm—either a wire needs to be adjusted or plugged back in." She reached into the incubator to assess the situation. "Let me attach this. There we go. Sorry to alarm you."

"Yes, the alarm alarmed me. Phew. Thanks."

Hannah's velvety, minuscule hand clutched my index finger. I wanted to rub and caress her silky, smooth head and back; however, Doctor Powers mentioned that micropreemies were especially sensitive to touch in the back and head areas. The predicament frustrated me, but I was never tempted.

The respiratory therapist stopped by to check Hannah's CPAP.

"Hello, I'm Erin. All is good with Hannah."

"Thanks, Erin. I'm Chris Hennessy, Hannah's dad. It's a pleasure to meet you," I said, and we shook hands. "It must've been a real challenge studying air in college."

She chuckled. "Studying the mixture of gases we cannot see, taste, or smell was quite interesting."

"That's cool, Erin-Air."

After that initial conversation, we had many short, uplifting chats. Erin was always sweet and friendly, and I always called her Erin-Air.

Each baby in this section of the NICU had their own primary nurse. Atina was Hannah's primary. We were in excellent hands. She was a mature twenty-four-year-old nurse and already a seasoned professional—competent, caring, and excellent at soothing our rattled nerves.

Atina came over and lifted the top cover of Hannah's incubator.

"What are you doing?" I asked.

"I'm going to clean Hannah's CPAP mask and change her diaper."

As she removed the CPAP and goggles, I was awestruck. *Hannah!* I saw her whole face and eyes for the first time. I wished Betsy were there to share the moment.

"Hey, soft-touch baby, it's your daddy. Mom and I love you so much. We're proud of you and your strength. Mommy and Daddy will help you win this battle."

Atina finished changing her diaper and said, "I'll place Hannah in your hands."

"Are you sure it's okay?" I asked fearfully. I didn't want to hurt her.

"I'm sure it's okay to hold your baby, Mr. Hennessy," she said, smiling. "Enjoy holding her for a moment."

She took Hannah out of the incubator, placed her in my hands, and snapped a picture of me holding my micropreemie, a one-pound-nine-ounce princess. I was infinitely proud.

However, watching our baby fight for her life was mental parental torture.

Atina placed Hannah back home in the incubator and left. *This isn't prison. It's a MASH unit on the front lines. We're at war.* I continued to quietly pray and sing to Hannah. "She's my little banana. She's my Hannah Banana. I want her. I need her. She's our little girl that Momma and I love."

Betsy and I established our approximate daily timeline protocol during the first week after Hannah's birth. We visited Hannah for an hour or more before 9 a.m., and Betsy was back at her side by 4 p.m. Betsy usually left around 8:00 p.m., and then it was just Hannah and Daddy until around midnight—sometimes later.

As soon as I arrived at Hannah's side, my hand went directly into the small hole on the side of the incubator. When my index finger brushed her minuscule hand, she grabbed it, and we remained connected until I left.

"She's my little banana. She's my Hannah Banana. I want her. I need her. She's our little girl that Mommy and I love." That was the number one song on the Chris Hennessy original song playlist that I softly crooned to Hannah hundreds of times. The combination of ad-libbed prayers and singing while physically connected was medicinal for both of us.

Those were arduous times, and although the connection with our baby happened three months before expected, Betsy and I never felt exasperated. We remained optimistic. I cherished the daddy-daughter bonding sessions Hannah and I had, and I sensed God's Spirit reassuring me that we would win this battle. I believed!

———

Two days after Hannah's birth, I got to the hospital at 6:30 a.m. Queen Betsy had been discharged that morning and was standing near the entrance with her belongings. I stepped out of the car and went to the passenger side. "Well, heavens to Queen Betsy," I sang like a Nashville honky-tonk singer as I opened the door. "It's lovely to have you back, Her Majesty," I said and bowed to my babes.

"My fabulous but peasant husband, please take me to our castle and prepare a fresh serving of shepherd's pie. I'm starved."

I couldn't help but chuckle. "My dear, I'm honored to transport you so you can quickly get ready, and we can go back and see our child." I placed her bags in the back seat. "We'll stop and feast at Whole Foods before seeing Princess Hannah."

"That would be sufficient."

We parked in our driveway eight minutes later, exited my car, and walked to the front door. Betsy looked up and smiled. "My sweet casa," she said as she reached toward paradise.

She unpacked, dressed, and made up her face. A few minutes later, we were in my car and chatted about Hannah all the way to Whole Foods. We sat and enjoyed a nutritious brunch before heading to the NICU.

Doctor Powers was at his office door, spotted us, and walked hastily in our direction. His body language projected trouble.

"Mr. and Mrs. Hennessy, I wanted to inform you of a situation. A brain scan early this morning revealed a tiny spot on Hannah's brain, likely blood from a stage-four bleed."

Betsy grabbed my forearm.

"We'll conduct a subsequent scan tomorrow morning. If the spot has grown, it indicates it's still bleeding." He paused. "In that case, the prognosis would not be good."

"Oh no!" Betsy gasped and came into my arms.

I held Betsy tight. "Can you explain in more detail?" I asked as my wife squeezed me.

"Intraventricular hemorrhage is a brain bleed most often found in babies who are born early. The smaller and more premature an infant is, the higher the risk for IVH. Infants born more than ten weeks early, like Hannah, are at the highest risk because blood vessels in their brains are not yet fully developed. They're very fragile as a result."

Doctor Powers sensed our traumatized vibes. "Please don't worry or panic. It could be nothing. Go about your day, and I'll call you tomorrow at 5 p.m. with the scan results." He looked at us, grinned, and left.

"This is another ride on our roller coaster to recovery," I whispered. "Hannah is going to defeat this. They said she's feisty. I wouldn't bet against her." I said it as if I believed it, and I did.

23

MY BLOOD CLOT SUSPICION AND HANNAH'S BRAIN SCAN

I drove to the Stanford Cancer Center for my appointment with Doctor Peterkin the following day. I noticed the oblivious folks in passing cars who had no idea how intense today would be for my family and me.

Several days ago, I'd talked to Doctor Peterkin about my swollen, black-and-purple foot and offered a self-diagnosis. "This must be a blood clot."

"Mr. Hennessy, let's not jump to any conclusions. Please be patient, and we'll see you on Friday."

I parked in the massive underground garage and limped up the stairs and across the street to have Doctor Peterkin examine my foot —the one I'd ignored for weeks.

I entered the office, and the medical assistant waited beside the receptionist. "Mr. Hennessy, let's take you right in." I followed her to a patient room. "Please remove your right shoe and sock. Doctor Peterkin will be in shortly," she said and left. Doctor Peterkin entered a moment later, and his eyes glanced down to my naked foot as he came to my side. "Did you injure yourself?" he asked with a wide-eyed look of astonishment.

"No."

"You didn't fall out of bed or walk off a curb without realizing it?"

"No. It began bothering me three days post-surgery."

He nodded. "I'm going to place an order for an ultrasound. Their office is across the street." He handed me the order, which included directions to my destination. "Head over there, and they'll take you right in. After the test, come back to my office."

I crossed the street and remembered that Hannah and I were both undergoing pivotal medical tests at the same time. *God, please let it be good news that Hannah's brain bleed is dry and not growing.*

I went in, and the medical assistant was waiting for me. "Mr. Hennessy, please follow me to the exam room."

We walked a short way, and she stopped at an open door. "Frank is your technician," she said, then smiled, turned around, and left.

"Hello, Mr. Hennessy. I'm Frank." The technician shook my hand as I entered a room lit by his computer screen and one fluorescent light. "I'll be conducting the ultrasound. Please remove your pants, shoes, and socks, and lie down." He pointed at the bed.

"Will it make noise?" I asked.

"No. Not a sound."

"Why call it ultrasound if it doesn't make a sound?"

"Hmm, I've never been asked that question," he replied and chuckled. "This imaging emits high-frequency sound waves."

"That sounds ultra-enough to me. Thanks."

He rubbed cream on my leg and started probing my groin area while intermittently looking at his screen. The desktop computer sounded like a Beatles record played backward in slow motion as the transducer slowly and carefully probed down the leg to right above my ankle. He repeated the same maneuvers on the left leg. "Okay, we're done. Please head right back to Doctor Peterkin's office."

"Are there DVTs?" I asked.

"You'll get the results shortly from Doctor Peterkin."

"Got it." I looked at the ultrasound equipment. "Incredible technology." I looked at the tech. "Thanks, Frank." And I hurried out of the dark room.

I walked across the street to Doctor Peterkin's office. *How did*

Hannah's brain scan go? I was concerned for my foot, but my mind and heart were with Hannah.

Doctor Peterkin seemed fascinated when examining my foot. "Mr. Hennessy, you were right on with your self-diagnosis," he said, looking at my foot like a kid discovering a new video game.

He looked up at me. "The ultrasound confirmed that there are two deep vein thrombosis blood clots in your right leg and one in the left. I'm so sorry. I rarely see this. I'm prescribing Warfarin, a blood thinner. You're going to have to—"

"Can I keep exercising? I'm walking three miles daily, and it's infinitely therapeutic."

He kept his head down and focused on my foot. "Please be patient and understand that DVT is a serious, life-threatening condition." He looked up. "If a piece from one of the clots breaks off and travels to the heart or lungs, it's called pulmonary embolism and could cause death."

"I understand."

"Let's give it two weeks to get the swelling down. At that time, we'll revisit walking. If all is good, movement will be fine because it helps with blood flow."

I grabbed the arms of my chair and was about to pull myself up and say thanks and goodbye, but Doctor Peterkin wasn't finished. "Because Warfarin typically takes a week to ten days to start working, you must inject a different, fast-acting blood thinner, Lovenox, into your belly for ten days."

No! I've been a sissy when it comes to needles since I can remember. I still turn my head when getting an injection.

"The nurse will show you how to administer your daily injection. When you leave, please head to the pharmacy and pick up your blood thinner prescription."

I wanted to get the Warfarin and go home, but I remembered Doctor Powers's words. "Hannah needs healthy, rested parents at her side." *This is life or death. Blood flow is partially blocked to my lungs. I must do it!*

"Hello, Chris," the smiling nurse said as she entered. "I'm going to help you with your Lovenox injections." She carefully took a syringe from the cardboard box, pulled the plastic top off the needle, lifted it, and showed me. "It has to be in the belly," she said gently. "You check for an area with loose skin at least an inch and a half from the belly button."

She pulled tummy skin and, with expert precision, thrust the needle into my flesh.

"Ow!" I instantaneously cried out in agony as an electric shock startled me and left me in severe pain.

"I must have hit a nerve." Her young face blushed. "It's a rare occurrence. I'm so sorry."

Hitting a nerve with a needle occurs once out of every twenty-five thousand shots. "No problem. I think I've got it," I said, then stood, turned away from her, winced, rolled my eyes, picked up my box of syringes, and left.

After experiencing the professional shot-giver, I had to go home and thrust the needles myself. It's something I needed to do, so I sucked it up and did it twice every day for ten days.

On the drive home, I felt sorry for myself and shed tears for several minutes. The entire right side of my stomach was bruised, like my ankle. Halfway into the drive, I let it go. The tears stopped, I resumed focus, and I changed my mindset to battle mode.

The Superman ringtone from my iPhone 3 interrupted the music I was listening to on my way home from Doctor Peterkin's office. I lowered the radio volume and pressed accept.

"I've been praying for you. Please give me the update," Betsy said sympathetically.

I didn't want to sound concerned, so I said nonchalantly, "There are three deep vein thrombosis blood clots."

"Oh no! Are you okay?" Betsy retorted with much concern.

"Honey, we knew what this was. I'll be fine. I can't exercise for two weeks as my body and the prescribed blood thinner begin working to dissolve the clots. Doctor Peterkin said that walking would be good after two weeks and would help with circulation."

"That sounds fine. How far away are you? I miss you."

"I'll be home in forty minutes. I can't wait to see you and Mom. We need each other right now. Let's have lunch together, and then I'll work in the office until Doctor Powers calls."

"Good plan. Mom and I are hanging outside in the gorgeous weather. Please drive carefully. We'll see you soon. I love you."

"I love you, too."

I stopped thinking of Hannah and myself and focused on my wife. Betsy was dealing with the reality that her husband and baby may not make it, yet she showed no sign of the relentless stress she'd endured for months. Fear and uncertainty had become our constant companions and the hope we clung to every day. I was the rock of my family, and Betsy was the boulder. We're one flesh. *Thank you, Father God, for sending her to me.*

I passed Pioneer High School, turned left on Ayrshire Drive, and then into the driveway of the fourth house on the left. Betsy and Mom sat on the front porch sipping iced tea. Betsy's mood was always exuberant when she was with her mom, which made me happy. I admired their relationship.

I stepped out of my sports utility vehicle. They stood, and Betsy walked to me, crying. We embraced. At that moment, I felt her love and support, which gave me the strength to face the challenges ahead.

"Baby, it's going to be fine. I feel great." I crouched and looked into those innocent blue eyes. "We're controlling the blood clots with healthy eating, hydration, and the blood thinner." I carefully drew her neck into mine and closed my eyes. As our necks snuggled, she settled down.

I opened my eyes and looked at their glasses. "Is that Mom's custom blend black iced tea?" I asked.

"Yes, it is," Mom said, looking at me. "There's a full pitcher in the freezer." She peered at Betsy. "Let's go inside and reload."

I opened the icebox, and the foggy cold air rushed out and

refreshed my sweaty face. I filled the girls' cups with Mom's blackest, tastiest iced tea. "You two should set up an iced tea stand out front while I work," I said.

"We'll make sure to put on sunscreen," Betsy joked, and we laughed.

I grabbed my frosty mug, filled it, and took a hearty gulp. "Mmm, the most delicious beverage—thirst-quenching with the perfect dose of caffeine."

"I love that my husband loves my mom and her iced tea," Betsy said, lifting her glass and smiling at me.

"It's going to be a productive afternoon," I said, touching Betsy's glass with mine. "To Mom's excellent mental-alertness blend." We toasted, and when that fresh, full-bodied brew rolled into my mouth and brushed my taste buds, the deep, pleasurable flavor delighted me as if I had discovered a fine wine.

We enjoyed hand-crafted tuna sandwiches on fresh San Francisco sourdough rolls, then walked from the porch into the kitchen, where we placed our cutlery and dishes in the sink.

"I reckon I'm ready for the office." I turned and walked through the hall, then stopped and made an about-face as I remembered my medicine.

"I need to take my second blood thinner shot," I said and grabbed the box of needles. Mom stepped into the living room as I pulled my shirt up. Betsy covered her mouth with her hands, which did nothing to muffle her shriek when she saw my bruised belly. "It was only severe pain for the first minute. It feels much better."

I removed a needle from its packaging. *I don't think I can do this.* I turned my head and told my mind to take a hike, pulled flesh on the non-bruised side of my stomach, picked up the hypodermic needle, and accomplished the shot.

"Great job," Betsy said.

"I'm glad I got it over with. Tomorrow it'll be easier. I love you," I said and kissed Betsy. "Have a great time with Mom. I'm going to get into my work."

"I'm proud of you."

"Why?"

"I know how much you hate needles, and you did it."

"Thanks, Bets. We've got this." I turned and walked through the hall and into my video production company's headquarters.

I found solace in being active, which helped me maintain a sense of normalcy amidst the chaos. I became wholly focused on editing a corporate video I co-wrote, filmed, and directed for OfficeMax, which helped my psyche. I'd have been a mental mess if I just sat around watching soap operas.

The next couple of hours flew by. If I had watched the clock, I'd have seen that time was moving in fast motion—it always does when I work creatively. At 4:47 p.m., my cell phone vibrated and jingled loudly, halting my session. It caught me by surprise and startled my soul. A spam call. *Ugh!*

My sympathetic nervous system triggered an acute stress response, and the resulting tension prepared me to fight or flee. Fight or flight is what it was like for cavemen every day. Thankfully, I wasn't alive back then.

I tried to resume work but was unable to concentrate, so I exited headquarters and went into the living room with Betsy and Mom. Our caffeine buzzes had waned. While Mom read the newspaper and Betsy texted with her best friend, Leigh, I closed my eyes and rested with Betsy's hand in mine.

At 5:08 p.m., my cell phone sounded off again. I scooped it from the coffee table lightning fast, like an NHL hockey player scooping the puck off the ice and slapping it into the net.

We were about to learn whether our baby had a life-ending brain bleed. Apprehensive energy churned throughout me. It felt similar to when I got butterflies while standing at the starting line of my high school cross-country races. Seconds before the starter fired his pistol, thoughts of the impending pain and suffering I'd tolerate during the three-mile race through mountainous terrain petrified me.

I placed my phone on speaker. Betsy and Mom hovered. Closing my eyes, I took a deep breath and said, "Hello."

Doctor Powers got right to the point. "Mr. Hennessy, it's good news. The spot on Hannah's brain has not expanded. It was a bleed, but it stopped. Hannah's brain is fine. I couldn't be happier for you and Betsy."

Fight or flight had flown from my existence. My eyes opened, and I ecstatically fist-pumped the air.

"Thanks so much, Doctor Powers. Feel free to call me every day with such news."

"We're all impressed with Hannah. She's a feisty fighter. I'll see you two tomorrow."

"Thank you, Doctor Powers," Betsy yelled.

"It's my pleasure, Betsy."

I pressed the red button, ending the call.

"Praise the Lord," Betsy's mom sang aloud.

Betsy shook her bootie and shouted, "Yippie!"

The three of us jumped up and down, yelling and woo-hooing. If a disk jockey had been present, he'd have started a conga line. It was a sweet and well-deserved celebration. Organic happiness is better than any man-made drug.

"Two Everest mountains have been conquered," I said as Betsy and Mom gazed at me, actively listening. "Hannah's lungs, brain, and heart are good."

"There's still a long route to recovery," Betsy acknowledged, "but let's enjoy this victory and the direction we're headed."

"Undoubtedly, we're going to walk out of that hospital with a healthy Hannah," I said.

God seemed to whisper to me, "Chris, keep it up. Trust me. These victorious battles will lead you and your family to triumph."

24

NICU NEIGHBOR BONDS

As we settled in our usual spots by Hannah's side in the NICU, Betsy's right hand found its way to a small opening on the incubator. Her extended pointer finger delicately touched Hannah's tiny hand, and Hannah's minuscule fingers instinctively grasped and held onto her mom.

"It's a miracle from God that we can connect with our precious girl like this," Betsy said, her wistful eyes watering. She looked at Hannah. "You are Daddy and me. Our love created you. We're family, and that is everything."

"That's so very well said. Thanks, Momma."

"I want to pick you up and hold you in my arms." She bowed. "God, please give us the strength and patience to wait until the time is right."

I heard a disturbance outside the NICU's maximum-security entrance. We were only fifteen feet away, the second spot on the right, when the door opened. A nurse wheeled in baby Sasha, Hannah's new neighbor, and placed her in the corner next to us. Her mom, Sandra, and another nurse followed.

Sasha was born on August 30, 2009, weighing seven pounds and eleven ounces. She didn't appear to belong in neonatal intensive care.

Looking at a newborn of that size in her incubator intimidated us NICU parents, who were surrounded by one- and two-pounders. Because we were used to guppies, Sasha seemed like a great white shark.

Any of the family members among the dozens of micropremature newborns fighting for their lives could grasp the horror of being in the Neonatal Intensive Care Unit. Our duress was elevated significantly. Even without having studied kinesics, we could tell by Sandra's body language that something heavy was going down.

"Chris, I'm so worried for those people," Betsy whispered. "The mom looks distraught. We need to comfort her."

Hannah lay next to us in her incubator, fighting for her life, yet Betsy had the desire and capability to reach out and comfort a total stranger. Betsy would be the first person in line to donate if a kidney transplant were needed, and she'd probably volunteer to prepare and deliver the recipient's dinner that same night. Her kind heart and fortitude made me proud.

Betsy slid her finger from the clutch of Hannah's hand and stood up. I followed her over to our new neighbors. Sandra quickly clasped Betsy's outreached hand. "Hey, I'm Betsy, and the tall, handsome guy is my husband, Chris."

"Hi, I'm Sandra." She turned to the incubator. "This is my baby, Sasha."

"Oh, Sandra, she's gorgeous," Betsy said.

"Thank you so much."

"That's Hannah," I said and pointed. "All one pound and nine ounces."

Sandra shuddered as she stared at Hannah.

"She was due December 7 and born September 1," Betsy said.

Sandra's head shook slowly in disbelief. "How is she doing, and how are you handling this?"

Despite the differences in our babies' conditions, we shared a common thread of hope and resilience. Betsy's words echoed our collective sentiment. "We're living in the moment, taking one day and one victory at a time. Hannah's climbing mountains and kicking butt, and seeing her and other babies like Sasha fight bravely gives us hope." In the NICU, we were not just individual families but a community bound by our shared experiences and aspirations.

"We're not used to seeing a full-term baby," I said, observing Sasha. "She looks like an NFL linebacker to us."

"Sasha is also fighting for her life," Sandra said and began to whimper.

Betsy embraced her. Sandra's eyes welled up with tears that trickled onto Betsy's shoulder.

After they pulled apart, Betsy asked, "Would you like to share about Sasha?"

"I noticed that with every attempt at feeding, she would gag and be very mucousy. She recently projectile vomited and then didn't want to eat. Our pediatrician assured me that occasionally babies develop a gag reflex because they swallow amniotic fluid. He told us that was normal. Meanwhile, Sasha remained calm and slept a lot, and I became pretty worried.

"Our nurse convinced the doctor to order a barium X-ray, which revealed a blockage. Sasha was diagnosed with colonic atresia —a rare, life-threatening intestinal obstruction. After we get settled, Sasha will undergo surgery."

I watched Betsy as she cowered in terror for Sasha while intently listening to everything Sandra said.

"We're so sorry. We're here for you guys," Betsy assured her.

Betsy will ask if there is something we can do.

"Is there anything you need right now?"

Sandra glanced down and then looked at Betsy. "Please call my mom and tell her what's happening and where we are. I tried her number several times this morning, but we never connected. She doesn't carry her cell everywhere, and the reception in here sucks for texting."

"Text me your mom's name and cell number," Betsy said. "Include her landline. I'll try her as soon as you leave. It'll be good for us to stay connected moving forward."

"Mom is my pillar of strength. She needs to be with us. Thanks so much, Betsy."

"You're very welcome. You may soon need to reciprocate, and I understand how much you need your mom. Having my mother's love and support has been priceless."

A nurse came in, followed by Sasha's surgeon, Doctor Dan Dotta.

The nurse asked Sarah to sign a form and then left.

"Doctor Dotta, these are Sasha's neighbors, Chris and Betsy Hennessy." She motioned to Hannah's incubator. "That's their daughter, Hannah."

"Hello, Mr. and Mrs. Hennessy. It's good to see you folks chatting and supporting each other." He nodded, looked at Betsy and me, and softly said, "Please excuse me. I need to have a word with Sandra."

Betsy and I went back to Hannah. Betsy kept her attention on her as I watched the doctor delicately explain to Sandra what he would accomplish during surgery.

If I'd focused only on the demeanor of that young, confident-looking surgeon, I'd have guessed he was about to take baby Sasha and her mom for a long stroll on the beach. I wouldn't have imagined that he was about to make several tiny incisions in an attempt to save Sasha's life.

Performing major surgery on a seven-pound baby seemed daunting, especially compared to operating on a one-hundred-eight-pound adult. The procedure was complex and risky, with only a 60 percent chance of success.

Doctor Dotta was obviously in a poised, carefree zone. He appeared laid-back like Betsy's dad when smoking his pipe and fly fishing.

As Doctor Dotta exited the NICU to prepare for Sasha, I wondered if he was as confident in his personal life. He could probably shuffle a pack of cards with one hand better than a Vegas card dealer using two. If I were betting, my money would be on Doctor Hero Hands.

Betsy reached out again to hug our new friend, and Sandra

instantly accepted Betsy's compassion. They clutched each other like two mothers with babies dangling between life and death.

"May I pray for Sasha?" Betsy asked.

"Please do."

"God, please give the surgeon full strength, concentration, and healing power. Let this begin a long, healthy, and happy life for Sasha. We thank you, God, and look forward to celebrating many happy birthdays together."

The nurse entered. "It's time for Sasha to be wheeled into the surgery room. Please grab your belongings and follow me."

Sandra picked up her purse and travel bag and smiled at Betsy.

"I'll call your mom. We'll pray for successful surgery and future times together," Betsy said.

"Thank you, Betsy."

The nurse wheeled baby Sasha to the doors, and Sandra followed.

"Walk tall, Sandra. God is with you and Sasha."

Sandra stopped, looked at Betsy, placed her hands on her heart, and said, "I love you, Betsy." Then she turned and walked through the doors as they closed.

While Sasha underwent surgery, Betsy connected with Sandra's mom, Lainey, and explained the situation. Twenty minutes later, Sasha's panic-stricken grandmother entered a new world. Fortunately, we were there to greet her.

"I'm Betsy. You must be Sandra's mom."

"I am," she said with a confused expression.

"We spoke on the phone."

She looked around, noticeably disoriented, and said, "Oh yes. Betsy."

A nurse opened the door and looked our way. "You must be Lainey."

Lainey nodded.

"I'm sorry they didn't have you stay at the front desk. Please follow me to the surgery waiting area. I'll update you on the way."

The nurse held the door. "Betsy, thanks for everything," Lainey said.

"You're very welcome. Sasha is in good hands, and Sandra is a strong mom."

Lainey smiled as the nurse released her hand from the doorknob. The door closed, and they hurried off.

Betsy's concern came back to Hannah and me. "Would you like a turn with Hannah?" I asked.

"I'd like to, but I'm exhausted."

"I didn't realize it was 8:15 p.m.," I said after looking at the wall clock. "You've had a long day, baby. Please go home and rest. I'll be with Banana for a couple more hours."

"That warms my heart. Thanks, honey. I'll head to the casa, shower, and go to bed."

"We love you, Mommy," I said. Betsy and I hugged and kissed, and she left. For the next three hours, it was Daddy-and-daughter bonding.

An adult male sitting among several one- and two-pound babies in incubators could have been the premise of a blockbuster Disney movie. The babies in charge learn that the father of the baby in the incubator near the front is helping to save her life, and they try to deflect distractions from an evil, full-term bully baby.

Hannah and I were without distractions except when the nurse or respiratory therapist made their rounds.

When a Daddy-and-Hannah session began, I'd reach into the incubator and softly say, "Hey, soft-touch baby, it's your big daddy." When her puny hand gripped my finger, I announced, "Babies and gentle folks, welcome to the Banana-and-Daddy show. Banana will be sleeping through the entire three hours of tonight's episode. I'll sing, pray, and talk to my stunning puny princess as she softly clings to my big daddy finger." The back of my tongue cupped the top teeth in the back of my mouth. I blew air through my throat, creating the crowd-cheering effect that I'd perfected by doing it hundreds of times.

The union of Hannah's hand and my finger was the ultimate intimacy; being unable to pick up and hold her was the ultimate frustration.

I serenaded her. "She's my little banana. She's my Hannah Banana. I want her. I need her. She's our little girl that Mommy and I love. That's love times two, and it's just for you.

"When we take you out of here, you'll see seas, mountains, trees, cars, and skies with planes and cotton candy clouds. You'll love our house and your room, which Mom and Grandma delightedly decorated after many trips to Pottery Barn."

Randi, the nurse I'd met, approached and said, "Mr. Hennessy, Hannah is a rock star. I'm so impressed with her tough, determined energy."

"Thanks, Randi. That means so much to Betsy and me."

"You're always the last parent to leave." She looked at the wall clock. It was 11:20 p.m. Betsy had been the most recent departure at 8:15 p.m. "Hannah's a fortunate baby." She pointed at an incubator across the way. "That baby has had no visitors, and she's been here as long as Sasha."

"What's up with that?" I asked.

"We don't know much. We don't even have a name."

I looked at the blank nameplate. "Was she abandoned?"

"No. She was born in week twenty-seven. I'll let you know when we learn more."

"Thanks, Randi. Is there any information on Sasha?

"Surgery was completed, and Sasha is in recovery."

"Thanks Randi. I'll see you soon."

"Good night, Chris."

It was 11:30 p.m. when I crooned one more time. "She's my little banana. She's my Hannah Banana. I want her. I need her. She's our little girl that Mommy and I love. That's love times two, and it's just for you."

25

KANGAROO CARE

September 8, 2009

I arrived at the NICU and Hannah's side at 6 p.m. Betsy had been with her since 4:10 p.m. Sasha lay alone in the incubator next to Hannah. Sandra was a nurse at a hospital on the east side of San José, working the swing shift.

"Sandra told me that Doctor Dotta was able to repair Sasha's intestinal obstruction," Betsy said. "It was too early to give a post-surgery prognosis. She's facing the possibility of several potential long-term complications, including mechanical bowel problems and feeding and absorption difficulties."

Atina came over from a nearby incubator. "Good evening, Mr. and Mrs. Hennessy." She smiled, not realizing she'd interrupted our conversation.

Betsy looked at Atina with a brief, polite smile. "Hey, Atina."

"Are you ready for a momentous and unforgettable experience?"

"Will our insurance cover it?" I asked straight-faced.

Atina chuckled. "I bet you've never heard of kangaroo care."

"When I was five, a kangaroo mob cared for me," I deadpanned.

Betsy glared right through me, which never stopped me from letting it out.

"Mr. Hennessy, you were probably the coolest buck in the mob."

"They called me suave Kangaroo Chris."

"Shush." Betsy slammed her pointer finger into her lips. "We need to hear this. Atina, please excuse us and continue."

"No problem. You two are the two most awesome parents ever." She looked at Betsy. "Kangaroo care is when you hold Hannah against your bare chest—also known as skin-to-skin care. It encourages bonding as well as emotional and physical development."

"This sounds fascinating," Betsy said. "Tell us more."

"Skin-to-skin contact is comforting and nurturing and will aid Hannah's recovery and development. It can reduce mortality, severe illness, infection, and length of hospital stay."

"We're in." I enthusiastically gave a thumbs-up.

"How does it work?" Betsy asked.

"You'll remove your shirt, then I'll take Hannah out of the incubator and place her in an upright position on your chest between the breasts. Does this sound like something you'd like to try?"

"Absolutely," Betsy and I said simultaneously.

"It sounds comforting and nurturing for the three of us," Betsy said.

"Yes, it is." Atina nodded her head in agreement. "Both of you and Hannah will benefit."

Betsy looked up with a strained face and placed her hands together. "This is an answered prayer." Her soft, blonde-streaked hair swirled toward Atina. "We had no idea tonight we'd be permitted to —" She paused, breathed deeply, and grabbed my shoulder. "Being able to hold our baby is something Hannah, Chris, and I need and deserve." She wiped her misty eyes. "I've envisioned this moment. Thank you, God."

I touched Betsy's face and gently gripped her precious head. "This is the best night of our lives."

Atina took Hannah from the incubator and placed her into the coziness of her mother's chest. She was still connected to wires and had headgear on, but we barely noticed.

"Reaching a finger to touch Hannah's hand is good, like when she's in the incubator," Atina reminded us. "Remember to refrain from making contact elsewhere."

"No hugging?" I asked.

"Not at this time," Atina answered.

Hannah melded into Betsy, and our little baby kangaroo slept soundly. Betsy beamed. "This is the first time I've had physical contact with my baby other than a hand through the incubator."

Hannah was about the size and weight of a six-week-old kitten. "How does she feel?" I asked.

"At first, I could barely feel her. Now, I can sense our fragile, tenacious baby and finally feel like her mom. Hannah's micropreemie heart must be wider than a mile. I wish I could hold her tight and caress her soft, silky head all night."

Betsy and I weren't thinking of climbing mountains, nor did we realize at the time that achieving kangaroo care was a new ridge reached for Hannah. We embraced and cherished the opportunity to be calm and present with our baby—many parents in the NICU don't get the chance.

"I need to be home with her," Betsy said while looking at Hannah.

"We are headed in that direction, Momma. There's no doubt."

"Betsy, time is up," Atina said after twenty minutes of skin-to-skin had passed.

Betsy smiled at me, then back to Hannah. "I don't want this to end."

I also wanted their time to continue.

"I'm sorry, Betsy," Atina said. "You'll do twenty minutes first thing tomorrow evening. Right now, it's Daddy's turn."

26

PICC LINE

September 10

Betsy and I arrived at 7 a.m. and took seats on opposite sides of Hannah's incubator. "Hey, soft-touch baby, it's your big daddy and best mommy," I said, then crooned, "She's my little banana. She's my Hannah Banana. I want her. I need her. She's our little girl that Mommy and I love. That's love times two, and it's just for you."

Doctor Powers walked through the entrance door, looked our way, waved, and disappeared into his office.

"What do you have going on today?" Betsy asked while Hannah's hand softly gripped her finger.

"The usual—answer emails, make follow-up calls," I said, "and edit a video. How about you?"

"I've got a packed schedule to see kidney patients and finish my assessment notes. I'll be home at 5:30 p.m. Let's do a walk-and-talk session."

"That sounds perfect. We'll meet at the house and then head to the trail."

"It's a done date, darling."

Betsy and I had recently shared our concerns about receiving potentially distressing updates about Hannah. During one of our walks, she bravely voiced, "We should be prepared for any challenging news or new issues that may arise."

"I agree," I reassured her. "It's important to be mentally prepared and ready to take immediate action if needed."

"Listen, digest, take a breath, and then deal with it."

"Well said. From now until Hannah's home, we must always be cognizant."

"It's easy to discuss out here on the trail."

"Be ready to handle bad news," I noted on my phone. "I'll write it out and add it to Hannah's health to-do list on the fridge."

"And we'll review it daily."

"We'll be ready to help Hannah," I said, and we fist-bumped.

Doctor Powers left his office and came by. "Good morning, Mr. and Mrs. Hennessy."

"Hey, Doctor Powers," I answered.

"It's good to see you," Betsy said.

"Likewise. Is this a good time to chat?"

Here we go again.

Betsy squeezed my hand. "We're good, Doctor Powers. Please, go ahead," I encouraged him.

Doctor Powers peered into the incubator. "Hannah's tiny, fragile arm has endured multiple needles." He looked at us. "There's a procedure that, if accomplished, would make it possible for Hannah not to have any more needles injected into her arm or anywhere else."

"I'd never thought about the needles," I said, looking at Betsy. "You?"

"No."

"No more pricks sound best for Hannah," I said.

"Instead of Hannah having to tolerate more needles, we'd like your permission to insert a PICC line."

"Insert what? Where?" I asked.

"Peripherally inserted central catheter, or PICC, is a unique IV inserted into the arm. The line is maneuvered so it carefully advances upward until the catheter is pushed into the heart."

Betsy shook her head, and I read her lips. "No way."

The thought of something being inserted into Hannah's heart, even for her own good, was shocking. It was like when the nurse looked up and said Betsy was nine centimeters and soon going to give birth to Hannah—even though she wasn't due for three months.

"Medicine is inserted into the PICC, preventing Hannah from enduring more injections."

"Yesterday, we added to Hannah's health to-do list on the fridge," I reminded her.

Betsy nodded and looked at Doctor Powers. "May I have a moment with Chris?"

"Absolutely," he replied.

Betsy and I turned and trooped to the back side of Hannah's incubator.

"This is the next worrisome Hannah issue like we talked about on the trail," I said.

"How should we handle it?" Betsy asked. "It sounds frightening."

"We also don't want Hannah getting pummeled with more shots. We should ask if there's a risk."

"Good idea."

"Doctor Powers, is there danger involved?" I asked when we returned to the front of the incubator.

"There is risk. A PICC can cause accidental puncture of an artery, nerve, or tendon. A clot may form around the catheter. An infection may occur near the insertion point. Unfortunately, the initial injection is quite painful."

"This sounds harsh," I said. "We're not sold on the benefits."

"The rewards far outweigh the risks," Doctor Powers said.

"There's a greater chance that continued injections will cause similar and even worse symptoms. PICC side effects typically depend on the person performing the procedure. The more experienced and proficient, the less likely complications will occur."

"May we ask who would perform the procedure?" I asked.

"Mary. She works like a magician and has eighteen years of experience. I trust her 100 percent," Doctor Powers reassured us.

We'd seen Mary in the NICU frequently but knew nothing about her.

"Please excuse me for a moment." Doctor Powers moved quickly to the other side of the NICU and returned with two nurses. "Belinda, we are considering Mary for Hannah's PICC."

"Mary is as good or better than anyone who has ever inserted a PICC," Belinda said.

June, the other nurse, added, "I concur. She could thread a needle with that PICC line into stone."

"Doctor Powers, what would you do if Hannah was your baby?" I asked.

"I would ask for Mary to get started immediately."

Betsy and I excused ourselves.

Despite our apprehension, we found the strength to make this decision for our daughter. We discussed the risks and benefits, our trust in Mary, and our belief that this was Hannah's best course of action.

"Honey, we should do this for Hannah. Think about all the needles she won't need to have. I think a PICC will save her arm from much misery. I feel God is telling us that Mary is the right administrator."

Betsy looked up at me, nodded, and consented. I wiped away her tears with a tissue, and we hugged.

"Let's go for it, Doctor Powers," I said with a thumbs-up.

"Very good." He turned and asked Belinda to summon Mary.

"You can both wait in the parents' room," Doctor Powers said. "The procedure will take approximately thirty minutes. I promise we'll take the absolute best care of Hannah."

The NICU's parents' room was private, comfortable, and an excellent place to temporarily escape the pressures of the NICU. It contained four tables with ergonomic chairs, one couch, a loveseat, and shelves with a decent selection of snacks and water bottles.

Betsy and I sat on the couch. She looked at a magazine as I counted seventy-eight bags of peanuts, thirty-six water bottles, and forty-seven power bars—and noticed my wife was gorgeous, even with a frightened face.

I grabbed a water bottle and a bag of saltless peanuts, walked to the back of the room, and stood at the observation window overlooking the incubators. They'd assembled a team of four medical personnel to accomplish the PICC procedure.

"It looks like they're about to begin." Betsy joined me at the window.

Mary peered at Doctor Powers, and he nodded. Then she acknowledged the team. Everyone was ready to proceed.

She picked up the needle and looked carefully at the contents.

"I can't watch this." Betsy turned away.

"God, please be with Hannah and her team," I prayed, feeling helpless.

We observed Mary position the PICC and then thrust it into our defenseless daughter's petite, puny arm. In obvious pain, Hannah wailed fiercely. It was the first time we'd heard her cry. The ferocious sound waves pierced through the soundproofed window and echoed across the parents' room.

"My Jesus, no!" Betsy cried out.

Hannah's anguished expression activated my inner anger. I needed to let it out. I squeezed my bag of peanuts and practically pulverized them into peanut butter. The bag popped open, spewing peanut pieces onto the floor. I turned and threw a half-full plastic-water-bottle fastball that burst upon pounding into the newly painted wall. Betsy ran to the kitchen area and threw up in the sink.

I regained my composure and went to help Betsy. I sponged her sweaty face with a cool, wet cloth, cleaned her mess, put my arm around her, and escorted her to the loveseat.

"Honey, let's sit and settle down," I gently said, and we sat shoulder to shoulder.

"That was horrifying," Betsy mumbled. "I want to be with Hannah."

"The worst is over. We did the right thing. Mary is doing her job. Everything is going to work out better for Hannah."

"I love you," Betsy said, snuggling her head into my chest. "Thanks for making me feel better."

"I'm proud of our teamwork in communicating with Doctor Powers. I love you, too. I'm going to check on Mary's progress."

Betsy picked up the magazine, and I returned to the window. Mary was focused on her work like a brain surgeon.

"Sandra!" Betsy screamed when our NICU neighbor dropped in.

"I thought you guys would be here. I saw a commotion at Hannah's incubator. What's going on?"

"They're putting an IV into Hannah's heart," Betsy answered.

"Oh my," Sandra said, taken aback.

"It's called a PICC. After the line is in, Hannah won't need any more shots. It seems like an eternity since they started."

"I'm so sorry. Is there anything I can do?"

"You're doing it by being here," Betsy said, and they hugged. "We're thrilled that Sasha's surgery was successful."

"Is Sasha experiencing post-surgery side effects?" I asked.

"Even though they repaired the intestinal obstruction, Sasha faces the possibility of side effects and issues for life. So far, she's eating well and pooping and peeing."

"We will pray for Sasha as long as we're alive."

The door opened. Doctor Powers strutted in and said, "The procedure was successful. Hannah has conquered another massive mountain."

We were relieved and elated but didn't jump for joy. The procedure had depleted us.

"Praise the Lord," Betsy said.

"Thanks so much, Doctor Powers." I stood and shook his hand.

Mary entered, and Betsy said, "You are Hannah's savior and our hero. We appreciate everything you've done for her."

"Hannah is gritty and determined. Her attitude is going to help win this battle. I hope I get to take care of her again."

"Such encouraging words are never forgotten," Betsy told her. "Hannah is our overcomer."

"Thanks, Mary. I'm sure we'll see you soon," I said.

Mary hugged us, then walked off to fight other battles.

I directed my attention to Sandra and motioned for her to join us at the window. "We want to show you something. See the baby across from Hannah and Sasha?"

"The baby with the blank nameplate?"

"Yes. She never has visitors, and the nurse said she's been here for a week."

"I've noticed. Was she abandoned?"

"No. She was born in week twenty-seven, and that's all they know."

"That's bizarre. Maybe the parents are ill."

"We'll eventually get an update. Until then, it remains a mystery."

Betsy, Sandra, and I visited with our babies for a few more minutes before heading to work. I sang, "Hann's a soft-touch baby, like outbreaks of snowflakes floating through the stormy sky. My heart has defrosted. We're here for you, my soft-touch baby."

27

NICU NEIGHBOR CRISIS: BABY THOMAS BRAIN BLEED

Thank God Hannah wasn't born on September 19, 2009. Betsy and I were scheduled to fly to the East Coast at 6:30 a.m. because I was slated to present an opening keynote for fifteen hundred video producers and filmmakers at the 2009 WEVA International Convention in Orlando, Florida. WEVA is the Wedding & Event Videographers Association.

Hannah would not have survived if Betsy had gone into labor in our airborne plane. If she had been delivered when we were in Florida—three thousand miles from Good Samaritan Hospital's highly regarded NICU—living would have been improbable. Immediate specialized care upon birth would have been imperative, and by the time we'd have arrived at a nearby hospital with a NICU, it would've been too late.

I canceled our trip on September 2, the day after Hannah's birth.

September 20, 2009

Thomas and his identical twin, James, were two and three incubators from Hannah. Betsy and I talked with their parents frequently. On the morning of September 20, a scan confirmed Thomas had a similar brain bleed as Hannah had recently endured.

"We're terrified about Thomas's outcome," his mother Katherine told Betsy, dumbstruck. "A follow-up scan tomorrow morning will see if the bleed is still growing."

"Hannah's bleeding stopped, and so will Thomas's," Betsy assured her. "We're here for you guys and will pray for Thomas."

"Thanks, Betsy. I really appreciate you," Katherine said and mustered a smile. "How did you handle waiting all day for Doctor Powers's follow-up prognosis call? We won't hear from him until 5 p.m. tomorrow."

"We lived life as usual and kept ourselves busy until 5 p.m. My mom and I had a fun mommy-daughter shopping excursion. Chris was working in his office when we got home late in the afternoon. It felt good to be together under one roof."

"I love that," Katherine said. "We'll certainly keep ourselves occupied." She lifted her hands into the prayer pose. "I'd hand over our house so that Thomas could get the same news as Hannah."

When Betsy and I entered the NICU the next day, Sandra sat at Sasha's side, staring straight ahead. Instead of popping up and exclaiming, "Betsy!" she looked our way and said nothing.

"Sandra, what's wrong?" Betsy asked.

Sasha's in trouble, I thought.

"It's tragic news. One of the twins didn't make it. Thomas was pronounced dead twenty minutes ago," she said, and her head sank.

"No!" Betsy cried out and put her hands over her face.

I closed my eyes and cringed. Sandra and Betsy looked at each other and burst out crying.

Thomas's subsequent CT scan disclosed his bleed was live and growing rapidly. Nothing could have been done. The medical instruments flatlined while James held his mom's pointer finger.

I knew that leaving the hospital and growing up without his twin brother would be a lifetime challenge for James. Twins share an irreplaceable lifelong bond—a sense of oneness that never goes away. James would likely always feel as if a part of him was missing.

"Why isn't there anyone consoling Thomas's parents?" Betsy asked, appalled. "Katherine and James Senior are sitting alone on the other side of the room." She looked into my eyes. "Those people need our love and support. Now."

Most wouldn't have the gumption to reach out and communicate with parents who had just lost their child, but Betsy rushed off, and I followed.

"Is there anything you need?" Betsy asked as we approached.

"Yes," Katherine solemnly whispered. "Please ask our primary nurse to take baby James out of his incubator. I need to hold him."

"I'm on it," Betsy said.

Katherine stood to thank her and then sat in the rocking chair.

Betsy scurried away to find their nurse. In twenty seconds, she arrived with Suchada, who removed the top of the incubator, carefully lifted baby James, and handed him to his grieving, distraught mother.

Katherine began an impromptu, skin-to-skin kangaroo session. She lifted her shirt, wailing, and placed James between her breasts. James Senior placed his arms around his wife and cuddled his family.

We walked away with our souls drenched in tears. It could have been Hannah, Sasha, or any infant in this unit. We needed to accept it and move on for Hannah.

NICU neighbors form lifelong bonds like soldiers in war. Others cannot grasp the connection without having the NICU experience.

One evening, after entering the unit, Betsy and I were startled to find that Hannah was not in her spot. We were too frazzled to notice that Sasha had also gone AWOL.

We hurried through the NICU, looking for our soft-touch baby. I stopped a passerby nurse and said, "May I ask if you could find out where our daughter is located? She's not in her usual spot."

"I'm so sorry." She picked up a nearby wall phone. "What's her name?"

"Hannah Hennessy."

She pressed zero and placed the phone to her ear. "Hello. I believe Hannah Hennessy was moved to a different location. Her parents are with me and anxiously await their daughter's whereabouts."

"Hannah's playing her first game of hide-and-seek," I said.

The nurse put her left hand over her mouth and chuckled, then turned her full attention back to the phone. "Okay, I got it," she said, hung up, and turned to us. "I apologize. We should have informed you of Hannah's new spot when you arrived."

"No problem," I said. "Please escort us to our princess."

"It will be my pleasure. Follow me." She turned to lead us, and Betsy and I trailed behind her into the next room, passing incubators and medical equipment. We rounded a corner. "There she is."

I noticed the handwritten HANNAH sign on the front of her incubator. Sandra smiled and frantically waved, and Betsy ran until they crushed into each other. "What a relief that we're all together," Betsy said.

"I arrived thirty minutes ago and screamed when I didn't see either of our babies. Atina escorted me to Sasha. I assumed we'd lost our neighbor. Then I noticed Hannah's incubator was next to Sasha on her left side instead of the right. I'd never been so grateful."

"They knew better than to move our forever friends away from each other," Betsy said, flexing her right bicep. They both punched the air and laughed.

"How is our forever friend?" Betsy asked Sandra.

"Sasha will likely be able to go home in about two weeks—she's a week ahead of schedule."

"That is fantastic news."

I enthusiastically agreed. "We're thrilled for you guys."

"I can't imagine not having you here with us," Betsy said.

"We live less than seven miles from here and less than that from each other, girlfriend. I promise you'll see me frequently until you guys are home with Hannah."

28

SKYROCKETING SUPPORT FROM
OUR CHURCH COMMUNITY

Hannah climbed from one pound nine ounces to two pounds nine ounces. She progressed at a steady rate, which was excellent news. However, she still couldn't tolerate her mom's breast milk—often referred to as "liquid gold" due to its nutritional value and the antibodies it provides. Once she was able to absorb Mom's liquid gold, she'd really thrive.

On Saturday, October 3, Lisa Averill and Cindy Sims, Westgate Church's children's ministry leaders, visited the NICU.

"The entire children's ministry staff, the children, and their parents have been praying for Hannah," Lisa said, reinforcing the deep personal bond we shared with our church community.

"Pastor Steve mentioned your story and prayed for Hannah during all five of last weekend's services," Cindy said. "Thousands of deserved prayers were lifted for you because you got involved in the community and spread love to so many families."

I peered at Betsy's dewy eyes and shivered in delight.

"Those prayers are very welcomed and needed," Betsy said. "Chris and I can't thank you enough."

"I'm in awe," I said, shaking my head.

"We are so proud of your love and caring for the kids and their families." Lisa handed Betsy a huge envelope. Betsy carefully tore the top off and pulled out a huge card signed by the kids' parents, which included colorful two-year-old crayon drawings.

"This is beautiful," Betsy said. "We miss our class."

I nodded. "Those little buggers have our hearts."

"Would it be okay if we prayed for you guys?" Cindy asked.

"Absolutely," Betsy and I said in sync.

The four of us held hands and bowed our heads while Cindy prayed. "Father God, Chris and Betsy truly love and care for the children on Sunday mornings. Their parents enjoy the service and learning your Word without worry. They know their kids are in loving, godly hands. Please return that same love and healing touch to the Hennessys."

"God, please bring them back to our community soon and in good health," Lisa added. Then she looked at us and said, "There's another gift inside the envelope."

Betsy reached into the envelope and took out a detailed meal calendar. It was filled with the names of church members who had volunteered to cook and deliver home-cooked dinners four days a week for the next two months. Their support not only provided us with a much-needed break from cooking but also ensured we could enjoy a variety of nutritious meals, which was crucial for our well-being during that challenging time.

"This is a blessing," Betsy said.

"It's a much-welcomed and needed windfall," I added.

They also planned and hosted a baby shower for Betsy. The girls enjoyed a fabulous lunch and each other's company. After eating, they presented Betsy with two big bags of like-brand-new, hand-me-down clothes for Hannah.

Abundant prayers also poured in from a new internet phenomenon—Facebook. I'd been on Facebook since the summer of 2008 and built quite a following during my diagnosis and cancer surgery. I found it therapeutic to compose and post stories describing our ordeals. My followers became captivated when I started sharing updates about our one-pound newborn baby.

The outpouring of love and prayers from thousands of Facebook friends and strangers provided us with emotional support and helped spread awareness about Hannah's journey, inspiring many others to join us in prayer.

Countless social media friends and strangers followed her progress. Many offered their love and prayers on my wall. Some even mentioned that their entire congregation had prayed for us.

"It's amazing how many lives our little soft-touch baby has touched and inspired while confined to her incubator," I told Betsy.

"She's such a superhero. We'll always respect her for the way she fought for her life without complaining," Betsy said. "I'm so proud of her."

Undoubtedly, the love, encouragement, and support we received from others was crucial in God's plan for Hannah's recovery.

October 17 was a sunny and pleasant Sunday with temperatures in the mid-seventies, but I hardly got to be in the beloved outdoors. Neither did Betsy and her mom. They had plans for a whole afternoon of shopping—searching for micropreemie clothes, which aren't easy to find. But those two were up for the challenge.

Hannah was too small to wear clothes for the first several weeks. We only needed to purchase blankets, diapers, and hats. The tiny diapers and hats she wore would fit comfortably on a bird.

While the women shopped, I enjoyed a long date with Hannah. We were finally free to take her out of the incubator and hold her. At 9:45 a.m., I arrived at the hospital, parked, walked quickly into the entrance, and took the elevator to the NICU.

"Hey, soft-touch baby, it's your big daddy," I said, slowly navigating Hannah out of her incubator. I carefully avoided wires and ensured the tubes stayed in place. The first time I tried, it was a disaster. Everything got tangled, so Atina rescued me. She unraveled Hannah while teaching me how to avoid playing Twister.

I held Hannah while sitting in a comfortable wooden rocking

chair. "Babies and gentle folks, welcome to the Banana-and-Daddy show. Banana will be sleeping through the entire episode. I'll sing, pray, and talk to my stunning puny princess and anyone else who wants to listen. Feel free to pray and sing along."

I chatted with parents, strangers, doctors, and nurses, and sang songs and prayed for Hannah.

A volunteer baby cuddler arrived at the lone preemie's incubator. She took the baby from the apparatus and held her for half an hour. Hannah didn't need such charity because Betsy and I were there for her several hours daily.

"She's my little banana. She's my Hannah Banana. I want her. I need her. She's our little girl that Mommy and I love. That's love times two, and it's just for you."

At 2:30 p.m., a nurse passed by and did a double take. "You're still here?"

"There's nothing I'd rather do than be with my baby. It's one of the best days ever, hands and butts down."

"It's beneficial and healing for both of you." She smiled. "Way to go."

"Thank you. Only one thing could keep me from leaving before 5 o'clock."

"What's that?"

"A hurting heinie," I answered, and we laughed.

At 3:05 p.m., I noticed my buttocks ached. By 3:15 p.m., I knew my boney butt could no longer handle sitting on that padless rocking chair. I stood and placed Hannah back into her incubator.

After holding her for close to five and a half hours, I opened the exit door and looked back at the lone preemie lying in her lonely incubator. I wondered how she was doing and where her parents were. *Thank God for the baby cuddlers.*

I turned and noticed the elevator had opened, so I hurried over and went through the slow-closing doors. The elevator took its time, and then the doors did the same when we reached the ground level. Betsy and Mom were standing there as I walked out.

"Hey, you two," I said. "You guys have that we-just-shopped-all-day look."

"We had a successful shopping excursion," Betsy said, showing me a couple of micropreemie outfits. Now, we're excited to see Hannah. Are you just leaving?"

"Yes, it was a day I'll never forget. I held her until I couldn't sit anymore. It's awesome to be able to snuggle her."

"Hallelujah," Mom said.

"Hannah has the best dad ever." Betsy hugged me. "I love you."

"I love you, too, Momma. Have a great time. I'll see you two this evening."

I started the car, feeling invigorated after being with Hannah. *I need movement.* I stopped at the trail and slowly stretched for several minutes, then walked a brisk three miles in sunshine and pleasant temperatures. I looked forward to later in the day when Mom, Betsy, and I would relax and enjoy dinner while discussing our day with Hannah. Then we'd watch *Dancing with the Stars* joyfully together.

29

FROM NICU TO IMPROV STAGE

Many males dirt bike, rock climb, ski off cliffs, and jump out of planes to fulfill their exhilaration needs. I removed the crud from the inner sanctum of my soul and reenergized myself by performing improv comedy.

My friend Jeff Werner and I, along with our fellow classmates, took a weekly improv class at San Francisco Comedy College during Hannah's ordeal. It was more than just a class; it was a needed getaway and outlet.

Jeff had suggested we look for a stand-up class, but I didn't care for performing stand-up comedy. It requires writing, testing, and perfecting your material, and is a tedious, time-consuming process. Performing the same material repeatedly wouldn't be stimulating.

Improv performances, however, are a thrilling dance with the unknown—fresh, new, unrehearsed, and primarily mental. Doing improv is like walking the plank over a cold, shark-infested ocean. The stage is the plank, and the audience is the sharks. When a topic is decided, nothing has been thought out or rehearsed. We wander the middle of the plank and speak words we concocted microseconds ago.

The sharks show their displeasure by throwing food and booing if we're not performing well or fast enough. Plummeting off a popcorn-filled stage doesn't compare to falling twenty-five hundred feet off the side of a mountain or a parachute not opening at ten thousand feet.

The last San Francisco Comedy College improv class featured our graduation performance in front of a packed house. My group's final topic was addiction, and someone in the crowd yelled, "Spoons."

The four of us had to perform an ad-libbed bit on being addicted to spoons. I cleared my mind and readied it for high-speed imaginative thoughts.

My teammate Charlie announced, "Welcome to another meeting of Spoons Anonymous. Chris, why don't you explain how you stopped using spoons."

"I purchased a bunch of used forks," I said instantly. When witty comebacks instantly materialize and are spewed rapid-fire out of your mouth, the hammerheads back off and show their approval with laughter. Enthusiastic crowd reactions lead to a more plentiful flow of hysterical improvisation.

Our bit closed when Miranda sadly said, "I miss spooning my boyfriend."

"Why don't you fork him instead?" I retorted, and the crowd roared. The emcee hustled on stage with music blaring and thanked us before moving on to the next group.

My improv performance was not just a form of entertainment but a way to stay positive and keep my spirits high during a difficult time. When the show wrapped up, I felt a surge of euphoria, like the runner's high I experienced when I took the silver medal in the 800-meter race at the 1974 New York State Track and Field Championships. I had a rush of endorphins, a feeling of accomplishment, and a sense of being on top of the world.

On the one-hour drive back to San José, Jeff talked nonstop. His brain ran like a machine that never needed rest. My brain was done. I wanted to tie Jeff to the roof, open my windows, and breathe the fresh, cool air while listening to music.

When I dropped Jeff off at his place, a half mile from Good Samaritan Hospital, his mouth was still going. I put my foot on the gas, waved to my buddy, and headed to the NICU to hang out with Hannah.

30

THE LONE PREEMIE: A STORY WITHIN OUR STORY

Betsy, Mom, and I were with Hannah most of the morning and early afternoon on Saturday, September 26. None of us visited the hospital that night. Instead, we enjoyed a rare night off watching television and resting before returning to see Hannah the next day.

My buddy Jordan and I had been trying to arrange for him to visit Hannah. That afternoon, it worked for both of us. He picked me up, and ten minutes later, we parked and walked to the entrance.

"You guys are lucky to live so close."

"I'm grateful that we're not the couple who drives daily from Los Banos," I said as we entered the hospital.

"Yikes. That's a two-and-a-half-hour round trip without traffic."

"It's a blessing our drive is only twenty minutes there and back."

"It gives you time to be with Hannah instead of multiple hours thinking about her in the car."

"Exactly. And multiple more hours singing to her instead of with the car radio."

"I'm sorry I haven't made it sooner."

"Don't be silly," I said, pushing the up button on the elevator. "I'm thrilled you've made the time and that Hannah is about to meet her

Uncle Jordan." The elevator doors split open, we entered, and I pressed the second-floor knob.

"Thanks, Henn. Uncle Jordan has never been in a NICU."

"That streak is about to end."

The elevator maneuvered through gravity to the second floor. "Are you nervous about the life-changing experience you're about to witness?" I asked when the doors parted.

"Yes."

I guided us toward the NICU, looked at my pal, smiled, and opened the entrance door. We slowly walked inside, and I pointed to the HANNAH sign. Jordan nodded and looked around, astonished. I went to Hannah, and Jordan witnessed as I placed my arm through the hole and into the incubator. Hannah's tiny hand grabbed and held my pointer finger.

"That was incredible. I've never seen such a minuscule human," he said, clasping my shoulder.

"The doctor said the best thing for Hannah is our touch, voice, and scent. I'm wearing my favorite moisturizer, talking, praying, and singing to her as she holds my finger for hours at a time. I believe Betsy and I are aiding in her recovery efforts."

"It seems insurmountable."

"We're 100 percent sure that Hannah is making her way out of here."

"If she doesn't make it, at least you still have Hadley, Harrison, and Hendrix."

I looked at my best friend and said, "Jordan, Hannah is alive, and we've bonded. We love her like my other three. If she doesn't come home, we'd be devastated."

Jordan perked up. It looked like he'd just come out of a trance, "Oh my. I understand. I'm so sorry for saying that, Henn. I'm an idiot."

"No, you're not, Jordan. Please forget it." That's how Jordan and I rolled. When one of us screwed up, we'd discuss it, forgive, forget, and move on with our relationship instead of holding onto it.

"I should have asked how she was doing."

"There have been no major setbacks. She's gradually improving, but there's a long way to go."

I grabbed a nearby chair. "Take a front-row seat and watch the Hannah-and-Daddy show."

"Very cool. This is what I've wanted to witness."

"Hann's a soft-touch baby, like outbreaks of snowflakes floating through the stormy sky. My heart has defrosted. We're here for you, my soft-touch baby."

"That was beautiful, Henn. I didn't know you could sing."

"Neither did I. I guess I can sing for Hannah."

"You're doing a heroic job." Jordan was dewy-eyed as I continued bonding with my soft-touch baby.

"She's my little banana. She's my Hannah Banana. I want her. I need her. She's our little girl that Mommy and I love. That's love times two, and it's just for you."

"After seeing only photos, this real-life perspective is fascinating. It's like watching a PBS documentary as it's being filmed," Jordan said.

"I'm glad you've enjoyed the show. Let's head home. I've got a date with Betsy and her mom."

"You're an amazing father, Henn," Jordan said as we exited the NICU. "That was an educational experience few ever witness. I'll always remember it."

"I appreciate that you took the time to be with us."

"Hey, Henn, I'm too invigorated to head directly home," Jordan said when we got into his car. "Let's drive to Stanford and walk the eighteenth hole of the Stanford Golf Course."

"Carpe diem. There's no super hurry. Let's do it."

Stanford Golf Course is located on campus below the scenic foothills about thirty-five miles south of San Francisco. It's consistently rated one of the world's finest courses. We drove north from the hospital and, in twenty minutes, passed the closed clubhouse and parked in the empty parking area. We exited the car and chatted while strolling to the first-hole tee box. The absence of other humans, the dusky sky, the chilly sea breeze, and the stunning view of San Francisco's skyline provided solace.

We strolled over to the impeccable eighteenth fairway—a narrow valley filled with luscious green grass and majestic, mature oak trees on both sides. I looked over at the San Francisquito Creek. A fox observed us like an interested crowd member watching a golf tournament.

Jordan pulled a preroll out of his pocket and lit it. We both took a couple of puffs of California's finest cannabis. Pain—and there was plenty of it—soon vanished and I felt pain-free and fabulous for the rest of the night.

"How are you doing, Henn?" Jordan asked.

"Right now, I feel great, Jordan."

"I mean overall. Hannah and your cancer. It's a lot to deal with, and I worry about you."

"I'm living each day as if nothing is happening out of the ordinary. It's working because I don't feel much stress or pressure."

"Hannah is progressing consistently and wonderfully," Jordan said, puffing like he was smoking a stogie. "You're fearless. I don't think I could handle such a situation."

"Thanks for those uplifting, supportive remarks," I said and smiled. "You'd be surprised what you can achieve. Don't ever under-estimate yourself."

We sauntered back to the car and barely spoke on the way home. Sometimes, being together and listening to music with those we care about is enough. Jordan dropped me off, and Betsy, Mom, and I had the rest of the night together.

On the morning of October 5, Betsy and I arrived at the NICU, and I sang to Hannah. "She's my little banana. She's my Hannah Banana—"

We stopped when we heard a beautiful voice singing along from the hallway. "I want her. I need her. She's the little girl that I love," Sandra caroled and walked into the NICU.

"Sandra, that was wonderful," Betsy said.

"How many times have you heard me sing that?" I asked.

"Infinity." She smiled. "It never gets old."

"Great job, sister," Betsy said.

"I agree." Betsy and I clapped.

"I have another song to sing," Sandra said. Then she belted out, "It came without warning. Sasha is headed home in the morning." Betsy and Sandra embraced and exulted.

"Way to go," I said. "We're so happy for you guys."

Betsy wiped off mascara tears. "We are ecstatic for Sasha."

"Would it be possible for you to drop Sasha off at home and then come back?" I asked. "I can't imagine Betsy being here without Sandra."

"We live minutes from each other and look forward to staying in touch," Betsy said. "You guys go home and live your lives. We're forever friends and look forward to staying connected."

"I'll definitely return frequently until you guys can leave," Sandra said.

Nurse Lori Smoke breezed in. "It sounds like a Mardi Gras celebration in here. What did I miss?"

"Sandra can take Sasha home tomorrow." Betsy pumped her fist with excitement for her friend.

"Going home are the best two words to hear in the NICU," Lori said, smiling. "Many congratulations."

"Hey, Smokeless." That's what I called her because her last name was Smoke, and she didn't smoke.

"What's up, Henn?" she asked, using the same nickname my friends called me in college.

"Do we have any information on the lone preemie?"

She nodded and gave a suave look, like a 1940s Hollywood actress. "Yeah, there's news that just came in this afternoon. Her mother was six months pregnant. She was driving her husband from their flat in downtown San José to Santa Clara University, where he studied electrical engineering. They had one car. She studied hospitality at nearby San José State, and they both worked as baristas at the Starbucks close to campus.

"A random shot was fired from an unidentified location. The bullet skidded through the left cheek of her young, beautiful face and lodged into the passenger seat. It wasn't a life-threatening injury.

"She lost control of the car, and it slammed into a tree. Both parents were airlifted here and declared dead on arrival. The doctors were able to perform a posthumous cesarean section and delivered the baby in her twenty-seventh week. She didn't have a scrape or a bruise and currently doesn't have a first name."

Betsy and Sandra stood static like the Tin Man did before getting oiled up by Dorothy and the scarecrow.

God, why? Please give us understanding and clarity. "They must have been a young couple."

"Twenty-two and twenty-three years old. The husband was to graduate in May."

The lone preemie lay there, not knowing she became orphaned before being born. Deep into the frigid, dark ocean, my heart sank like the Titanic.

She was a gorgeous baby with soft cheeks and a smooth head like Hannah's. I reached into her incubator, picked her up, and held her. "You're not being neglected. You had two loving parents striving to care for you and give you a good life. Now, you're a micropreemie orphan laying in a lonely incubator."

As we mourned and shed tears, Doctor Powers came over. "We'd wondered about this baby, and Lori explained her situation," I mentioned.

"We've never experienced such a tragedy," Doctor Powers said, shaking his head.

"What will happen to the baby?" Sandra asked.

"We don't know."

NICU is not fun. I wanted to go home with my wife and baby.

31

HANNAH'S NON-RESPONDING DIGESTIVE TRACK AND MY MAGICAL MYSTERY TOUR

Hannah was flourishing and appeared headed toward recovery. Since late October, she'd been taking Betsy's liquid gold breast milk from the tube that runs through her nose, down the esophagus, and into her stomach. Our soft-touch baby was gradually and steadily gaining weight. There had been no major medical obstacles to impede her progress.

"I'm a bit concerned," Atina mentioned when we arrived at Hannah's side on November 2.

"Why is that?" Betsy asked.

"Hannah hasn't pooped for two days."

"She's been pooping every day."

"Yes, she had been."

"She took two days off. The poop will come out tomorrow," Betsy confidently sang.

When we arrived the following evening, Betsy asked Atina, "Sunny or cloudy?"

"Cloudy," Atina answered and made a sad face.

"Should we be concerned?" Betsy asked.

"Not yet. We must continue to wait and hope."

"And pray."

Hannah went four more days without defecating. When Betsy and I arrived at her incubator, I picked her up and said, "Hey, soft-touch baby, it's your big daddy." And then I announced, "Babies and gentle folks, welcome to the Banana-and-Daddy show. Tonight, Hannah will do an enormous poop as I sing, pray, and talk to my stunning puny princess while changing her wonderful dirty diaper."

I changed two diapers. Both were moist and slightly yellow without anything resembling poop.

Ten more poopless days went by for a total of seventeen. We were worried times infinity.

"Mr. Hennessy, our tough little Hannah's digestion issue has returned," Doctor Powers said. "I'm so sorry. We've taken her off Mom's milk. A urinary tract infection has also been diagnosed."

"Is her life in danger?" I asked.

"Hannah's life has been in danger since birth," Doctor Powers answered. "It's a miracle that she hasn't experienced more setbacks."

"What's next?" I asked and grabbed Betsy's hand.

"We'll scan her digestive system to check for a blockage. A dye will be placed in Hannah's feeding formula, and we'll follow it through the stomach and digestive tract. If we see even the slightest movement, the culprit is slow motility caused by her digestive system not being fully developed. If there's an obstruction, Hannah will have to endure major surgery like Sasha."

Betsy squeezed my hand. "When can we expect the results to populate?"

"Tomorrow."

"Thank you, Doctor Powers," she said.

I wished him a good night, and Betsy and I left.

We'd arrived in separate cars, so before I got in mine, I said, "I'm headed on a magical mystery tour," and we hugged heartily. That was a phrase I often used to describe an emotional escape. "I'll see you at home in about an hour and a half."

Betsy knew I would chauffeur myself to a favorite getaway by the Santa Teresa Hills, which separates our neighborhood from Almaden Valley. It's a delightful drive through a charming community. The houses on the south side of the street have backyards leaning up the hillsides. I drove unhurriedly with the windows open, soaking up the fresh air and blaring music.

A private road splits off to the right and dead-ends a hundred yards up at the base of the hills. I occasionally make an impromptu night-time stop and take in the panoramic views of Silicon Valley below, with shimmering lights on the ground and the Diablo Mountains standing tall as a backdrop. That evening, I left the car and hung out, reveling in the music. The vista looked like something my Silicon Valley neighbor Thomas Kinkade would have painted.

It was a spectacular November night—cloudless, windless, and sixty-two degrees. I turned away from Silicon Valley, and my eyes appreciated the perfectly round, luminous moon dazzling in the crystal-clear black sky above the hills.

Soon, the movement of our rotating, blue, marble-looking planet with white swirls would cause our blazing white moon to retreat behind the hilltops.

The tunes amplified my already magnified mood. A song I listened to on repeat began with a low, slow, mystical-sounding keyboard. Transcendental vocals morphed in and paired with a powerful melody. The piece gradually built until there was a pause— a turning point that suddenly erupted into an upbeat, punk-rock-like surge of energy before fading to an extended, soft, hazy, dreamlike ending. That tune moved me and stirred my emotions time after time. I cranked the audio and sang with fervor.

Suddenly, a magnificent shooting star, followed by an exceptionally colorful streak of light, passed by the moon and disappeared behind the hills. *Wow!* One moment later, the moon also vanished. I didn't want the show to end, but the universe is on its own time schedule.

That was a sign. God has heard thousands of prayers for Hannah. If we continue to pray, persevere, and live life as usual, the fight for brightness in our lives will be won. We were determined to see Hannah's and my issues sublimely depart like the moon and the shooting star, inspiring us to keep battling and staying positive.

I returned to my car and drove the five minutes home with renewed spirit and focus. I felt reassured and confident in our journey, convinced Hannah would soon recover.

The quart-sized mason jar, a constant reminder to stay adequately hydrated, sat on my desk. I was engrossed in work on the desktop computer when Betsy's call interrupted my focus. As I reached for the phone, my hand knocked over the entire glass of water. *Ugh!*

Betsy's voice came from an unknown location. "The results came back negative. It's not a blockage!" I heard her say, and then I saw my phone lying on the floor in a puddle of reverse osmosis water. I picked up the drenched phone, and Betsy continued, "They believe that her digestive tract is still developing and that things will soon move normally."

"Yes!" I exclaimed, jumping to my feet and pumping my fist like Tiger Woods does after sinking a winning putt. We've conquered the final mountain, baby!"

When we arrived at the NICU the following day, Atina greeted us with a good report. "Hannah did a huge poop—a total blow-out."

"I'm completely blown away," I said, and we laughed. Laughter was a welcome change after the tension and worry we'd experienced.

"That's the best news ever," Betsy said.

"The doctors are very encouraged by Hannah's progress. I'm so happy for you guys." Atina smiled and turned toward me. "I've yet to change her diaper, Dad."

"I'll gladly do the honors," I said, feeling joyfully over the moon—way past it like the shooting star. Removing Hannah's filthy diaper and then wiping her tiny, stinky butt, and putting on a clean, puny diaper was my pleasure.

Hannah fought hard, and we'll always admire her inner strength. "It's like God is holding her hand," Betsy said. "I'm so proud of her for not letting go. She's going to win this battle."

I agreed. We both believed all the prayers had been crucial.

Betsy left for home, and I stayed and held Hannah for an hour before returning home to the office.

After several harrowing days, Hannah completed a remarkable turnaround. Her weight climbed to four pounds and three ounces. The infection was gone. Her digestive system functioned properly, and her eyesight and physical therapy readings were normal.

Kaye, a regular night nurse, came by frequently to chat. Her adorable classic southern Alabama drawl proclaimed, "This baby wants to suck."

Confused, Betsy asked, "What does that mean?"

"When a baby weighs more than four pounds and wants to—and can—suck, it means she's ready to go home," Kaye said and removed Hannah's feeding tube.

I don't know whose smile was bigger—Betsy's or mine. "That's music to our ears. When we get out of here, I'm writing a song titled, 'This baby wants to suck.'"

Betsy offered Hannah a small bottle of breast milk, and Hannah sucked it down like an experienced baby-bottle drinker. Betsy patted her softly on the back, and soon, a loud burp made the three of us laugh.

That tube was never again reinserted. Goodbye intravenous feeding, hello all food by mouth.

"She's better off at home now," Kaye said.

"Why is that?" Betsy asked.

"An infection for Hannah at this point could be fatal. She's much more at risk in this place." Kaye explained how being at home was safer than being in the hospital with all its germs. "Now, let's get her out of here."

32

NICU GRADUATION DAY

We had yearned for Hannah's release date to be around mid-December. After nurse Kaye's observation, our team announced that Hannah would likely be able to come home during Thanksgiving week. It was Sunday evening; Thanksgiving was in four days.

The next morning, Doctor Powers opened his office door and approached us with a smile on his usually stoic face. "Mr. and Mrs. Hennessy, we're confident Hannah is ready to leave the NICU and live an amazing life. Congratulations."

I raised my hand, we slapped five, then Betsy and I jumped up and down like we did when Doctor Powers told us that Hannah's brain bleed hadn't progressed. The relief and joy were overwhelming, and tears of happiness streamed down our faces.

"We're going home!" Betsy exclaimed.

"The three of us," I said.

"Woo-hoo!"

"Would you both be able to meet here tomorrow at 10 a.m.?" Doctor Powers asked. "It's customary for me to lead a processional for departing families through the unit to say their goodbyes."

"A parade!" The thoughts of that thrilled me. "How fun!"

"Yes, we can both be here," Betsy answered.

"Good. We'll see you then."

On Tuesday, November 24, Betsy, her mom, and I got in the car for our final trip to the hospital. We didn't hurry or stress. Hannah's battle to live for the first three months of her life resulted in victory.

"Our prayers have been answered," Betsy said as we were en route to take possession of Hannah. She put her hand on my shoulder, bowed, and prayed, "Father God, thank you for the finest ending to an arduous journey." Tears dampened her stunning eyes. "Chris and I have acquired the strength, knowledge, and experience to be right-eous parents. Thank you."

We parked at Good Samaritan Hospital for the last time and strolled to the entrance.

"What's going on, Mommy?" I asked Betsy as I filmed with my professional video camera.

"My baby girl is coming home," she said gratefully. "This is our Christmas, New Year's, and every other holiday combined."

"How is Mommy feeling?" I asked.

"My emotions are overflowing." She shook her head and held back tears. "I can't—"

"We can't talk right now. It's too emotional," Mom said, and we meandered through the automatic entrance doors.

I waved to the security guard, and we traversed down the hall and through the closing elevator doors. When they opened, they revealed our last odyssey into the NICU entrance. Walking in there as a newbie parent had been daunting. But witnessing Hannah's consis-tent determination and resilience—and the teamwork among Betsy, me, and the medical staff—molded us into better, more vital, confi-dent folks.

Atina met us at Hannah's incubator. "Here's the first step in leaving the NICU," she said before removing the wires connecting Hannah to the monitors and computer, forever detaching our baby from the Neonatal Intensive Care Unit.

Betsy signed several papers that we'd never look at again. I picked up Hannah and held her wirelessly for the first time. Carrying a disconnected Hannah was like frolicking freely through the Alps as the von Trapp family celebrated their freedom at the end of *The Sound of Music.* We didn't need the green grassy slopes, majestic mountains, or background music. Having Hannah was all that mattered.

Hannah's parade began with Doctor Powers leading Betsy, Mom, Hannah, and me through rows of incubators. We passed our comrades, the babies, and their families we had to leave behind, and the loving nurses who are our forever heroes. The atmosphere was a mix of bittersweet farewells and hopeful beginnings, with each nurse and family we passed offering their congratulations and best wishes.

"You're a very loving father," a nurse said.

"Thank you," I responded, and we hugged.

Nurse Suchara was next. "That's a tough kid. We knew she'd make it. Much mazel tov."

"You wonderful folks made our jobs easier," another added.

"Your positive outlook and love for Hannah were inspiring."

Mary, who had inserted the PICC line, said, "I had no doubt there'd eventually be happy goodbyes. I'm so proud of Hannah, and you should be too." Her words echoed in our hearts, validating our little girl's strength and resilience.

"Thank you so much, Mary," Betsy said, and they embraced. "You and Hannah are both superstars."

Lori Smoke directed her comments to me. "Thanks for making us all laugh when we felt like crying." She could barely get the words out before breaking down in tears.

I heard someone in the distance shout, "Go, Hannah!"

It was a whirlwind tour through the front lines. "Betsy, let's leave before they change their minds."

Doctor Powers brought us to the exit doors and said, "Hannah's entire physical and mental being have experienced significant hardship and trauma since birth. It will take several more months for her to recuperate fully."

"Thank God she'll be in the comforts of her home," Betsy replied.

"Yes. Home is best. The NICU isn't a pleasant place. Thank you for boosting this unit and putting smiles on our faces. Your attitudes, love, and support undoubtedly helped Hannah survive. Go do great things together."

"Thanks, Doctor Powers. You're a gentleman and a total professional. This was a team effort." I was determined to not let my emotions get the best of me. "You listened and explained each situation thoroughly and understandably. Betsy, Hannah, and I will forever thank you and respect you and team NICU."

Atina accompanied us downstairs to the lobby. "Atina, your competent, stressless demeanor kept us calm and composed during those terrifying first days. We looked to you for guidance and support, and you pulled through every time. Betsy and I think you're awesome. I'm so proud of what you're doing at such a young age. Keep up the good work, kid."

"We'll always remember and tell Hannah about Atina," Betsy said.

Atina opened her mouth, but nothing came out.

Betsy and I hugged her, and then she turned and walked out of our lives.

I ran outside the sliding glass doors and prepared to capture the monumental moment on video. As I stood there, I felt a sense of closure for the past and anticipation for the future, a mix of feelings that defined this significant moment in our lives.

Betsy hauled Hannah in the baby-carrying basket, and Mom walked by their sides as they passed through the doors into the open air.

"This is our baby's first time outside after spending her first three months in the hospital," I excitedly exclaimed to a few people waiting to go in.

A pittance of moments out of nearly forty million in our lifetime are unforgettable. That was one of them. Even if I hadn't filmed it, it would still be forever playing in my mind.

We exuberantly paraded Hannah into the parking lot and to our automobile, ushering in a new era of transportation for her.

I filmed inside the car as Betsy placed Hannah in her oversized car seat. Our next stop was home. Betsy drove, and I sat next to my champion, Hannah. We left that familiar parking lot for the last time. The car ride was filled with relief, joy, and peace about the new responsibilities that awaited us. We had climbed mountains together —now we were headed home, my family and me.

33

TWO YEARS LATER: AN UNEXPECTED DOCTOR CALL

Hannah had transformed into one of the healthiest kids in San José and was about to turn two and a half years old. A woman who was with her child at the play area in Whole Foods remarked, "She's big for two."

No, she's not. She's a micropreemie. I smiled and remembered that Hannah was no longer a micropreemie, then peered at our flourishing daughter playing with the woman's toddler. "Thank you."

Betsy and I took the next day off, headed over the Santa Cruz Mountains to the Pacific Ocean, and left behind hundreds of thousands of Silicon Valley techies doing their technology jobs. It was a seventy-degree weekday in mid-February, and I liked that the sun leaned away from Earth in winter. The rays hit us at an angle that provided ample sunshine but wasn't overly bright like the harsh summer sunlight.

We hiked down a steep winding path, carved through the cliffs, to our favorite beach at Seascape Aptos Resort, twelve miles south of Santa Cruz. We pranced through the cool sands and claimed a spot near the water far enough away so our towels and shoes wouldn't be carried off to Hawaii.

"Let's keep moving," I said. My family and I walked the shoreline toward Monterey. The mighty ocean was on our right, and the beautiful bluffs and the vast sandbox that weathering and erosion created were on the left. The long, sloping strip of luscious sand had seashell fragments sprinkled in. It reminded me of the sprinkles Sweet Retreat Creamery placed on Hannah's ice cream cones. Hannah held a colorful, smooth seashell.

Betsy's and my health and work were prospering, and Hannah had morphed into a rosy-cheeked, full-of-life toddler. The three of us held hands while we enjoyed our family time until a ringing cell phone startled us and disrupted the tranquility.

Where was the receiving party of this phone call? The nearest humans were at least two football fields from us.

"It sounds like it's coming from your butt," Betsy said, and we laughed.

I reached into my pocket, grabbed my ringing phone, and looked at it with a weird face. It was family time. I hadn't planned to bring the phone onto the beach. I thought I'd left it in the car.

The caller? Stanford Cancer Center. I hesitated but eventually answered.

"Hello?"

"Mr. Hennessy, it's Doctor Peterkin from Stanford Cancer Center."

"Doctor Pee Pee, I miss you. How are things at Stanford?"

"Yes, Mr. Hennessy," Doctor Peterkin said, "all is fine. I wonder if this is a good time to discuss your quarterly blood test."

I had done a follow-up blood test the prior week to check my PSA levels. They'd been conducted quarterly until three months earlier when my results showed a slight rise from .03 to .05. At that point, Doctor Peterkin told me, "There is no cause for concern. This is a very slight rise. To be certain, we'll start testing monthly."

My next PSA reading was .08.

"Your current PSA is .10. When your PSA has risen three consecutive months, it indicates prostate cancer is still present. I'm so sorry."

My heart sank. Doctor Peterkin's words hit me like a wall of seawater. "Before leaving the hospital, you told me the pathology report was clear. You said you got all the cancer," I cried out.

Betsy figured out what was going down and started sobbing. When Mommy cries and Daddy is upset, your not-quite-three-year-old knows something terrible has happened. Hannah also began to cry.

"Occasionally, a tiny amount of cancer isn't detected on X-rays or scans after escaping the prostate gland before surgery," Doctor Peterkin answered.

"That's wonderful," I said sarcastically. "You've made my day."

"You need to—"

I cut him off mid-sentence. "What does this mean?"

"You're now dealing with advanced prostate cancer."

I looked at Betsy and Hannah. "Was I really voted the most handsome patient ever in Stanford Hospital C-2?" I asked, smirking. "That's epic." I made a funny face and rolled my eyes before taking a few steps to distance myself from the girls. "Doctor Peterkin, I'm with my family at the beach. We'll continue this conversation next week."

"That's good. You can call for—"

I pressed "end call" and raised my head. From where I stood at the top of a slanted slope with Betsy and Hannah below, closer to the water, I appeared to be seven feet tall. They looked up at me, frightened.

I turned and noticed paragliders jumping off the magnificent cliffs overlooking the massive ocean. The cool, refreshing breeze perfectly combined with the blazing blue sky and warm, delightful sun rays. A massive spray of delicious, refreshing salt water pelted us.

I looked at my soaking-wet iPhone 5, turned toward Hawaii, heaved my beloved device with all my might toward Maui, and shouted, "Goodbye, Doctor Pee Pee!"

My cell phone plopped into the ocean and disappeared. I faced Betsy and Hannah and laughed. "I promise everything is going to be fine. I love you guys more than any cell phone or anything." I turned, ran at full speed, and leaped into a chilly, crashing wave. The fifty-five-degree curative sea water invigorated my bones, nerves, and muscles, and the potent burst of energy thrust me out of the water and back to my girls.

"Daddy wet," Hannah said.

I picked up my princess and carried her into the water, placing her up to her lower belly. She laughed and screamed loudly. "Daddy, it's cold."

We left the water and went back to Betsy.

"Let's race, Hann," I yelled and sprinted a freezing fifty-yard dash. I stumbled and fell into the sand. "Hey Hannah, I'm the sandman."

Hannah arrived and jumped on top of me. We tumbled around, and I tickled her. She looked into my eyes and said, "I love Daddy."

It was as if her heart were speaking words through her mouth. "I love you, too, baby," I said, putting my hands on my chest, "with all my heart."

I didn't think about tomorrow or the next day. The only thing that mattered were those precious moments together.

Standing, I grasped Hannah's left hand, and Betsy held Hannah's right hand. We had epic things to do together, like skipping through the hallowed sands of the beach, singing, and not fretting about anything except having the best time ever.

Betsy and I did exactly what we wanted and needed—simultaneously being physically and mentally touched by Hannah.

"It was likely a microscopic amount of cancer that eked its way out of your prostate before surgery," Doctor Peterkin said at our follow-up appointment. "We know it's there because your PSA levels are rising, but it'll take some years before it shows up on a scan."

"How many years?" I asked.

"Maybe five to ten."

"Is there anything I should do in the meantime?"

"Continue your healthy lifestyle. We'll check your PSA quarterly and do a yearly scan until the cancer shows up on the radar."

"What happens when it shows up?"

"We're excited about the development of less harsh treatments that could keep the PSA down and eradicate cancer. New types of radiation therapies will be able to pinpoint and zap the cancer, and softer hormone therapies are being tested and perfected."

"That's great, Doctor Pee Pee," I said. "Please tell them they've got five to ten years to get it right."

"You've got it, Mr. Hennessy." Doctor Peterkin reached out his hand. He looked straight into my eyes during our long, firm handshake. "Thanks for being a great guy. I feel sorry for the cancer. It won't like putting up with you and your outlook."

"Thanks for your kind words. They mean a lot coming from you."

I drove home in a yin-yang state of mind, untroubled and relaxed.

Our church congregation's unwavering support, from prayers to practical help, comforted me and strengthened my resolve to fight. Their show of love reminded me that my family and I were not alone in this battle.

Introducing a holistic doctor to my medical team was a significant step. With fifteen years of experience treating cancer patients, Doctor Huynh offered extensive natural treatments and counsel. His focus on diet, herbal medicine, and lifestyle recommendations—all aimed at enhancing the body's natural ability to combat cancer—instilled a profound sense of reassurance and hope. His treatments not only complemented the traditional medical approach but also empowered me to take an active role in my healing process.

When I was initially diagnosed, Doctor Jack told me that attitude was everything. At a later appointment, he marveled at my ability to entertain and have his staff and patients laughing. "Mr. Hennessy, this behavior can help boost your immune system more than 20 percent." His words served as a powerful reminder of the impact of a positive attitude in the fight against cancer.

Doctor Powers had acknowledged my impact on the NICU, lifting the grim atmosphere and helping Hannah make it alive.

As a confident man and father who persevered and learned much during Hannah's and my battle for life, I knew I could handle any challenge. I vowed to conquer cancer and inspire and motivate others facing similar challenges, igniting a fire of faith and determination in each of us.

The cancer pushed me to pursue and realize my dreams. I had no fear, worry, or doubt that I could continue being Hannah's best daddy. God assured me I could enjoy life while reaching my potential.

I moved on, thankful to be alive and thankful for having Betsy and Hannah. Today, I continue to live in the moment—life as usual.

EPILOGUE

First Times: Hannah's First Adventures at Home

December 2009

When you persevere through life's most challenging times, you emerge stronger—as people and as parents. Each small victory builds confidence, creating momentum that carries you forward. One accomplishment leads to another, until you find yourself capable of tackling anything life presents.

Our Touched by Hannah journey transformed Betsy and me in precisely this way. After months of medical uncertainty, beeping monitors, and measured hope, these simple firsts became our celebration of life itself. Working from home allowed me to spend countless hours with Hannah—not just watching her grow, but truly experiencing each precious moment of discovery alongside her.

Our First Back-to-Back

When your baby comes home after spending the first three months of her life in the hospital, you don't want to let go. We held Hannah. A lot.

At night, we nestled our soft-touch baby between our tired bodies. My two hands easily held Hannah's precious entirety.

One cold winter night, I lay awake, concerned. We were in the grips of the Great Recession. My video production business was tanking. No money was coming in. The future looked bleak.

"What am I going to do?"

At bedtime, I can usually shrug off all worries until tomorrow—a gift I never take for granted. That night, I struggled.

Hannah seemed to sense my distress. Instinctively, she squirmed her tiny, warm body against the curve of my spine, melding perfectly into place. It was remarkably comforting. I drifted off to sleep.

When I told Betsy, she dubbed the position 'back-to-back.' 'Back-to-back' became part of our distinctive family language. A solid 'back-to-back' night between any of us was always a good night.

Hannah's First Outdoors Walk

Hannah wasn't supposed to leave the house for six months. It was December 12—only three weeks after Hannah came home and a few days after her actual due date, December 7, 2009.

I researched whether fresh Pacific air might benefit Hannah's health. Late afternoon winter temperatures in San Jose (upper 50s to low 60s) were pleasant, and studies showed that people who spend time outdoors breathing clean air have stronger immune systems.

I decided to include Hannah on my daily three-mile walks—just Hannah and Daddy. Our first trek on December 13 was a highlight of my life. The late-afternoon sunshine and windless 58°F temperature were conducive to walking. Hannah wore the cutest lamb-like furry onesie. At about five pounds, she fit easily in the Baby Bjorn.

The Baby Bjorn was remarkable for bonding. Hannah's tiny body slipped through the harness against my chest, her ten precious fingers interlaced with mine. We faced each other, her gorgeous little head at my neck level, that petite face with chubby pink cheeks looking content, peeking out of the hood.

Betsy waved goodbye, and off we went into our Cambrian San Jose neighborhood. I talked gently, nonstop. After walking for two blocks, Hannah's half-open eyes slowly closed. I'd never witnessed such a tranquil creature. She stayed asleep, and we held hands for the remaining 2.9 miles. My heart overflowed with pure joy.

First Bird, Tree, Dog

Hannah stayed awake longer on each walk. I noticed her growing awareness of our surroundings. One day, mid-hike, I turned her to face outward in the Baby Bjorn. She looked up, captivated by leaves blowing in the breeze. A bird landed on a tree branch and took off. Hannah's head followed. "Did you see that, baby? That's a bird, and she can fly!"

I ran, jumped high, and flapped my arms like that little bird— probably looking like Big Bird from Sesame Street. "Let's fly away like the birdie, okay, Hann?"

A woman and her dog strolled toward us. "Hello, may I pet your doggie?"

"Sure. She's very friendly. Her name is Wilma." I reached out, and Wilma licked my hand several times. Then I placed Hannah's hand near Wilma, who rapidly kissed Hannah's hand with wet bullets of love.

"Wow," the owner said. "She loves your baby."

"Of course she does," I replied. "That's Hannah Hennessy," and winked.

Dad's First Friday, March 5, 2010

As Hannah settled into life at home, we established new routines that became an essential part of our family life.

Friday became my favorite day. Betsy's maternity leave ended, and her employer generously allowed her to work a four-day week with the same pay and benefits.

Betsy's mom drove four hours round-trip from Davis every week, caring for Hannah on Mondays and Tuesdays. Mom would leave early Wednesday afternoon, and I had Hann the rest of the day. Betsy had Thursdays off. Friday was my turn for all-day daddy duty.

My first Friday with Hannah was a fairy tale. No work, schedule, or worries—just Princess Hannah and King Daddy all day.

Hannah was sleeping when I said goodbye to Betsy. Ten minutes later, she woke up and saw Daddy at her crib's side. She probably became conscious because I was standing there waiting for her to wake up.

As I changed her diaper, I asked, "Hey, baby, did you have a good nap?" She smiled with all her heart. It took a few minutes to change her diaper. I never stopped talking, and Hannah never stopped smiling.

I picked her up and we held each other tight. We walked into the kitchen, grabbed a bottle of mommy's golden milk from the fridge, and sat on the comfortable couch in the living room.

Witnessing Hannah guzzling that entire bottle was such a blessing compared to those initial tiny 5cc droppers we hoped she'd take back in the early NICU days. When finished, she let out a huge burp that left me in disbelief that such a loud sound could come from a small baby.

First Ice Cream, August 2010

By summer, Hannah was ready for bigger adventures.

Driving past a local strip mall, I noticed long lines outside Sweet Retreat, a small ice cream shop. A thought came—Hannah was ready to experience ice cream.

For a quarter, the guy gave me a small scoop on a cone. Perfect for Hannah. She sat on my lap. It was evident that she fell instantly in love with that sweet, creamy, frozen combination. She also chewed on my wallet, seeming to enjoy it almost as much as her ice cream.

She went back to her ice cream and swallowed a small spoonful. Suddenly, Hannah's happy face cringed in pain. Before I could react, the pain vanished, and she continued to enjoy her treat. Hannah had just endured her first brain freeze.

Most of the chocolate ice cream made it into her mouth. The rest formed a temporary brown tattoo across her face.

There was a Taekwondo club four stores away from Sweet Retreats. We walked there and looked through the window. Hannah was mesmerized by twelve kids in bright white uniforms with black belts doing synchronized head-height kicks while yelling, "Hi-Yah!" The instructor waved us in to take a look. Hannah sat on my lap, and we watched for several minutes.

After-dinner ice cream outings became an hour or two of daddy-daughter bonding. When Hannah finished her treat, she'd mumble "Hi-Yah" and point the way. "Hi-Yah" became a regular part of our ice cream expeditions.

Before going home, I'd place Hannah in the driver's seat while I stood outside watching her pretend to drive. She loved the controls and gadgets, grabbing change from the ashtray and stuffing it into my CD player. I watched her explore, resisting the urge to intervene. My CD player was never the same, but Hannah's sense of discovery was worth more than any electronic device could ever be.

These afternoon adventures became our ritual. Each outing brought new discoveries, and I learned to see our neighborhood through Hannah's curious eyes.

Flowers and Messes

Hannah and I headed for a long walk on a gorgeous San Jose morning. About a mile from home, we came upon a small house surrounded by beautiful vines, bushes, and flowers.

When I held Hannah's face up to a cluster of bright purple potato bush flowers, looking at them wasn't enough. She reached out instinctively, gently touching God's creation. Then suddenly, she thrust the flowers into her mouth. Her focused expression changed to, Ew, how could something that looks so sweet taste so sour?

I laughed and plucked the plants from her mouth.

A woman emerged from the house, saw Hannah surrounded by her floral friends, and presented my baby with a small bouquet. Hannah grasped it tightly until our next stop—CVS, where I needed to pick up a prescription.

I grabbed a rubber ball in the toy aisle, threw it high, and caught it. Hannah's eyes followed the entire flight path, and the flowers slipped out of her hands. Her mesmerized face filled my heart with joy. I played more catch with myself, and Hannah laughed with delight.

I put her down, and she crawled straight to the colorful boxes. I filmed with my iPhone as she pulled herself up, grabbed toy boxes, and heaved them onto the floor without looking back at her work. Then, she went off to the next shelf to continue her mission of destruction.

It was wonderful. Boxes of toys and games filled the aisle like a sea of presents under Christmas trees.

I picked up every box and put them back in place before we left. Other shoppers gave me looks—some disapproving, others amused. I could have stopped her with a sharp "No!" but watching her pure delight in exploration felt more important than a tidy aisle.

The video got several thousand views on YouTube. Viewers mostly offered love and laughter, praising me for being a swell dad. Some viewers were shocked that I allowed Hannah to have so much fun. One commenter wrote about boundaries and spoiled children. Another replied, "I would have loved to have a daddy spoil me like that and love me so much." It's intriguing how differently we humans see things.

Anyone who meets Hannah notices a loving, creative, confident, happy child who isn't spoiled with material possessions. I believe I'm providing her space and freedom to explore and create—parenting that will help develop her imagination.

Our explorations weren't limited to walks. Every errand became an opportunity for Hannah to experience something new.

First Lollipop

At Walgreens, I spotted Tootsie Pops and remembered childhood visits with Hannah's older siblings twenty years prior. We'd sit on the small wall surrounding bushes and play "flip the coin" while enjoying our treats.

Hannah sat in that same spot, literally sucking the sweetness from her first lollipop. She climbed over the wall into the dirt, playing with handfuls of earth that slid through her fingers onto her head and shoulders. She wasn't deterred when her face became filthy.

When she put a handful of soil in her mouth, it sprinkled over the Tootsie Pop, which created a priceless sour expression. Some parents might have panicked, but I knew she was learning through experience—something no amount of warning could teach her.

I also knew the benefits of Hannah playing in nature. Experiencing millions of bacteria and microorganisms is necessary for developing a healthy immune system.

These messy moments of discovery led us to other simple pleasures I'd forgotten could bring such joy.

First Carousel Ride

I spotted a small four-horse carousel. There was a magnetic field pulling us to the coin slot. I placed Hannah on a horse's back, dropped in a quarter, and turned the lever. The music began, and horses started galloping. My soft-touch baby was going round and round all by herself—a sight that awed me. There were many more quarters spent on that ride.

As Hannah grew more comfortable in the world, I wanted her to experience the warmth of community as well. That's how we ended up making Starbucks part of our routine.

Hannah with Dad at Starbucks

The guys were delighted to finally meet Hannah at my go-to Starbucks. Big Joe yelled, "Coffee is on me today, Henn!" He became Hannah's adopted Christian uncle.

Hannah sat on my lap, watching Daddy socialize with his buddies, relishing in free therapy that I loved and needed. It became apparent that Hannah also enjoyed being around people.

When barista Keanna held Hannah, my baby bawled loudly enough for McDonald's patrons across the street to hear. While distracted, Hannah grabbed my half-cup of coffee and dumped the contents on my lap and the floor.

How did I react? I laughed. This wasn't the first time I'd chosen patience over control. Throughout our adventures—whether she was pulling toys off shelves or eating dirt—I'd learned that harsh "no's" shut down her natural curiosity. She was too young to understand rules, but old enough to sense my energy.

I preferred that Hannah not think she was constantly misbehaving, so she rarely heard the word. Instead of harsh "no's," I gently explained each individual situation. Too many curtly delivered negatives are detrimental to creative and emotional growth. I wanted Hannah's creativity to flourish.

These first times—walks, ice cream, flowers, carousels—became the foundation of our bond. Each moment taught us that love, patience, and the freedom to explore make the most ordinary experiences extraordinary.

ACKNOWLEDGMENTS

My dear Uniondale High School friend Deborah Howell suggested the perfect title, *Touched by Hannah*. I'm so grateful we reconnected on Facebook after all these years.

Author Chess Desalls reviewed my paragraph of words and came up with a brilliant subheading: A man with cancer. His one-pound newborn. And their fight for life.

The love, support, and invaluable feedback from my social media followers sustained me throughout this twelve-year journey.

Thanks to my HennSchtick on Substack followers: your readership and encouraging feedback meant everything.

The California Writers Club provided dozens of enriching seminars and crucial networking opportunities that shaped my growth as a writer.

A chance encounter at the California Writers Club Sacramento branch led to a pivotal connection. Pete Cruz, author of the award-winning memoir *No Tears for Dad*, mentioned me to New York Times bestselling author Cecil Murphey—a connection that proved transformational.

Thanks to Cec Murphey for your tough love, old-school discipline, and for pushing me to become the writer I aspired to be. I will be forever grateful.

Bernard Wozny, then president of California Writers Club Sacramento, generously spent hours across multiple sessions walking me through the IngramSpark independent publishing platform.

My deepest appreciation to Twila Belk for meticulous proofreading and insightful suggestions; Dr. Katherine Hutchinson-Hayes for always being there and providing expert consultation; Karen A. Phillips for her stunning book cover design and unwavering professionalism; Sue Trowbridge for flawless formatting; and Shawn Langwell for his expertise and honest, invaluable feedback.

Thanks to Kim Edwards for consultation on the back cover text and Gini Grossenbacher for her spot-on consultation and indie publishing wisdom.

Fellow Cecil Murphey protégés Rodney Combs and Lilka Raphael offered crucial insights that helped my prologue shine.

Thanks to my in-laws, Denny and Stephanie Walter—I call you Mom and Dad out of love and respect—for being the best grandparents and in-laws anyone could ask for.

Thanks to my Dad, James Hennessy, for the ridiculous humor and lightning-fast wit you instilled in me from an early age. Mom, you weathered Dad's antics with grace and have always been the best mother.

Finally, thanks to Hannah and Betsy for loving and supporting my journey completely, and for trusting me to keep Hannah's memory alive.

ABOUT THE AUTHOR

Chris Hennessy is an award-winning filmmaker, author, and speaker who continues achieving remarkable creative success while battling stage IV prostate cancer since 2020. With over 6.8 million combined platform views, including 4.1 million on his Hennflix YouTube channel, Hennessy builds his audience through social media, his monthly HennSchtick newsletter, and speaking at writers' conferences, industry symposiums, company conventions, business events, and corporate summits nationwide.

A Rice University graduate, Hennessy spent nearly three decades (1990-2018) producing 1,500+ professional films for major clients including Google, eBay, and the SF 49ers. Since retiring, his creative output has only intensified.

Hennessy's television series *Yolo YoYo's* won Best New TV Cable Series, 2019, Access Sacramento, with 125,000 Facebook views (TV stats not available). His documentary *Miracles on College Street*, a Yolo YoYo's episode created to promote his memoir *Touched by Hannah*, earned the "Film Heals Award" at the 2022 Manhattan Film Festival and was runner-up for "Best Episode West Coast" at ACM Western Region WAVE Awards.

Chris Hennessy, Hannah Hennessy, Grandma Stephanie Walter, Grandpa Denny Walter, and Betsy Hennessy, Easter 2025

Hannah Hennessy on a mission trip with Anthem, June 2025

www.ingramcontent.com/pod-product-compliance
Lightning Source LLC
Chambersburg PA
CBHW060130130626
46556CB00006B/2296